CU00646211

ABOUT THE AUTHOR:

Helen L. Conway is a solicitor with Mace & Jones Grundy
Kershaw in Huyton, Merseyside. She specializes in family
work and particularly work with victims of domestic
violence. As part of her law degree at Hull University and
her M.Phil from Trinity Hall, Cambridge, she completed
theses on domestic violence. She sits on the Domestic
Violence Forums for Liverpool and Knowsley and for a
short time was a volunteer for the St Helens Women's Aid.
Her articles on domestic violence and other Family Law
matters have been published in various legal journals as
well as magazines such as *Parentwise* and *Choice*.

Jennie
Fytche
01778
42162

For my Grandad, Herbert Eric Causey.
I miss him still.

Domestic Violence: Picking up the Pieces

Helen L. Conway

A LION BOOK

Copyright © 1997 Helen L. Conway
The author asserts the moral right
to be identified as the author of this work
Published by
Lion Publishing plc
Sandy Lane West, Oxford, England
ISBN 0 7459 3722 5
Albatross Books Pty Ltd
PO Box 320, Sutherland, NSW 2232, Australia
ISBN 0 7324 1584 5
First edition 1997
10 9 8 7 6 5 4 3 2 1 0
All rights reserved
A catalogue record for this book is available
from the British Library
Printed and bound in Great Britain by
Caledonian International Book Manufacturing Ltd, Glasgow

Acknowledgments

No book is ever written without the indirect influence and direct assistance of other people. I would like to extend my thanks to the following:

Martin Parry of the University of Hull encouraged my interest in this subject and Martin Edwards, probably unwittingly but nevertheless effectively, gave me the inspiration to start my writing again. Also, the belief shown in me and the encouragement given to me in tough times by my best friend has been invaluable.

The book could not have been written without the confidences of the people whose stories are used in the book. Open Door Counselling in Liverpool and Mike Wilson provided invaluable material for the counselling section. The training programmes run by St Helens Women's Aid and those run under the auspices of the Knowsley Domestic Violence Support services by such groups as Sefton's Women's Aid, the NSPCC and the Liverpool Probation Service all added to my understanding of the subject. Various members of the Merseyside police domestic violence units have also taken time to explain their role to me. My Granny's recounting of her own childhood experiences gave me the opening for the book.

Finally to my husband, Dennis Woodcock, who has never failed to encourage me and who has painstakingly proofread everything I have produced.

Contents

Introduction

One summer afternoon Aileen (not her real name) left the home of the relatives who cared for her and went to visit her parents in their Edinburgh tenement block. These visits were not always pleasurable. Her father—once an army bandsman—had been injured in the service of his country and was now unemployed. Often he was to be found in the pub, where he would invariably take more than the one drink which was all it took to arouse his temper. His wife would remain at home, caring for the younger children in this large family and struggling to make the family income stretch to meet their needs.

It was not unknown for Aileen's father to assault his wife, although on the whole this was kept from the children. However, this was not always very successful—Aileen was only thirteen when she saw her mother with black eyes after one of his assaults. On this day, when she arrived at the flat, she found her mother barricaded in the back bedroom. Her father, worse the wear for alcohol, was hammering violently on the door and demanding that she let him in. Aileen gathered her younger siblings together. They watched in fear, knowing that if their father did get into the room he would undoubtedly beat their mother again.

Aileen, as the eldest, took charge and shepherded her brothers and sisters down to the neighbour's flat below. Desperate for help they begged the neighbours to intervene to get their mother to safety. The sounds of their father's rage echoed down the stairwell of the flats. Time was running short. The neighbours turned the children away.

'Sorry,' they said. 'It's a family matter—it's not for us to interfere.'

Domestic violence is not a new problem. Aileen was in fact my own grandmother. Her father joined the army at the age of fourteen after his own parents abandoned him. He was shot in the shoulder in 1917 in Mesopotamia. The violence continued through the depression in the 1920s and 1930s until he secured work in 1939 when the younger, fitter men were sent to war.

Nor is domestic violence only a problem of the past. Having written two university theses on the topic, I now work as a solicitor specializing in family law and can see several women a week who suffer from violence at the hands of their partners. Statistics show that as many as one in four women may have experienced at least one incident of domestic violence in their lives.

For many years domestic violence happened but was ignored. Then in 1971 Erin Pizzey founded Chiswick Women's Aid, the nation's first refuge for battered women. The significance of this went far beyond the practical help she was able to give to women in her locality. It was the start of a campaign which seeks to spread the message that domestic violence is not acceptable and must be stopped. This campaign is continuing today as more and more agencies learn about the terrible and far-reaching consequences of abuse in the home.

The problem still exists but today there is a strong message of hope which can be given to victims of domestic violence. There are places of safety to flee to. There are people who will listen and believe. There are churches which will support and not condemn. There are laws which will protect. There are ways in which broken lives and shattered relationships can be rebuilt.

This book is aimed at those who are suffering from domestic violence and people who may know someone in that position or wish to help such victims. Research shows that most victims are women. However, one of the consequences of the developing campaign against domestic violence is that it is becoming more and more apparent that men can be abused too. This book refers to victims as women simply to avoid the cumbersome necessity of having to refer to both sexes throughout. However, as the section in Chapter 2 states in greater detail, the book is equally for male victims and they should not feel excluded by the choice of language in this book.

Throughout the book are examples and quotes from people who have been through the experience of domestic violence. Many of these are drawn from clients I have acted for in the past. Others have been passed on to me by other people working with victims of domestic violence. In all cases every effort has been made to protect the identity of the women involved and to maintain confidentiality where the information was given to me in a professional capacity. This means that names and identifying details have been changed where necessary. However, nothing has been done to distort the examples given. The names may be fictional—the suffering is only too real.

I hope that this book will help people to understand domestic violence more—to realize how deeply it can affect victims. I also hope that those who have been abused will find in this book a message of hope. The book does not just describe the horrors of being trapped in an abusive relationship; it aims to show a victim the way out.

CHAPTER 1

Hidden wounds

Debbie went to see her doctor with a badly bruised back. Her doctor was concerned about how it had happened and gently drew the story out of her. Her husband had come home drunk, as he frequently did, and had smashed up some of the furniture in the hall. When she objected he pushed Debbie against the banisters and spat in her face. She admitted that he behaved like that quite often. Sometimes he would swear at her for hours on end. Other times he would grip the tops of her arms so tightly that she would lose feeling in her hands. On occasions he had locked her in her bedroom while he went out for hours at a time. Her doctor explained to her that she didn't have to live that way and that there were organizations who helped people suffering from domestic violence. Debbie was surprised.

'But it's not domestic violence!' she said. 'He has never hit me.'

There is no simple definition of domestic violence. The term 'domestic' is used to indicate that the violence occurs in a personal relationship. Often this is between husbands and wives or people who are living together. However, sometimes the definition is extended to include other family relationships. For example, there is increasing concern about so-called 'granny bashing'—abuse of elderly people within the family. At other times the couple involved may have a close relationship but not actually be living together. This book concentrates mainly on violence between adults who are in a personal relationship of whatever kind, but some of the content will also be relevant to other instances of family violence.

Defining the term 'violence' is even more problematic.

Obviously, it can include a whole range of physical acts which would commonly be accepted as violent. This could be:

slapping
punching
thumping
burning
biting
kicking
attempted strangulation
shaking or 'ragging'
pushing someone down stairs
stabbing.

However, acts of domestic violence can also include physical acts which are more unusual. It is perfectly possible for a woman to be a victim of physical domestic violence without ever actually being hit by her partner. There are many other forms of physical abuse which women have been subjected to, such as:

being put in a bath of cold water and being scrubbed by the abuser until the skin bleeds
being tied up or put in chains
having bags being placed over their head or being gagged
having weapons held against them
being made to sit absolutely motionless while the abuser spits at them
being forced to use drugs
having cigarettes stubbed out on them.

Other forms of violence can be sexual in nature, such as:
being forced to have sexual intercourse against their will
being forced to allow the use of implements in intercourse
being subjected to anal intercourse against their will

being forced to dress up or perform acts which they
consider to be degrading

being forced to have intercourse while other people
watch

being forced to use or watch pornography.

However, all these physical acts are, unfortunately, only part
of the story. Domestic violence also covers a whole range of
other behaviour which exerts power and control over the victim.
This is why the alternative term 'domestic abuse' is sometimes
used to express how wide-ranging the issue really is. One writer
even expressed it as 'conjugal terrorism'. This non-physical
abuse can often accompany physical violence, or it can come as
a precursor to physical violence as a part of the build-up to the
assault. However, in some cases there may be no physical abuse
but a long pattern of emotional abuse. This form of domestic
violence is not to be underestimated. It is often this type of
behaviour which causes the most damage. Physical violence
may leave scars or bruising which will heal over time—even if it
takes years. Emotional abuse, however, can leave deep but
hidden wounds which can easily go without treatment, leaving
the victims hurting for years to come. The after-effects of this
type of abuse can change people's personalities and make it
difficult for them to live a full life in the future without help and
support.

There are several kinds of abusive behaviour, which are often
pictured diagrammatically in the form of a wheel (often called
The Duluth Wheel—see the diagram opposite). This diagram is
commonly accepted by such organizations as Women's Aid as
being a good way to show how the physical and sexual violence
is supported by the emotional abuse which happens inside the
wheel. The hub of the wheel is the power and control which is
the aim and outcome of the violence and abuse.

Physical   VIOLENCE   Sexual

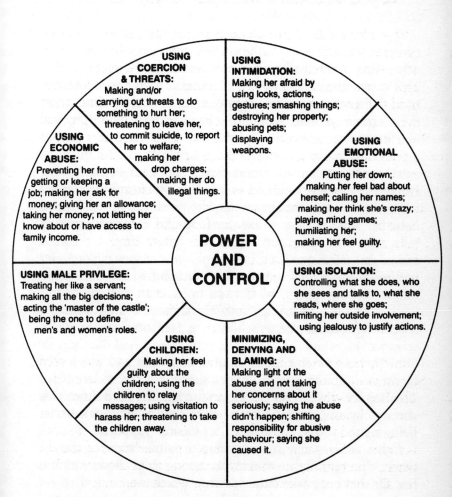

USING COERCION & THREATS: Making and/or carrying out threats to do something to hurt her; threatening to leave her, to commit suicide, to report her to welfare; making her drop charges; making her do illegal things.

USING INTIMIDATION: Making her afraid by using looks, actions, gestures; smashing things; destroying her property; abusing pets; displaying weapons.

USING ECONOMIC ABUSE: Preventing her from getting or keeping a job; making her ask for money; giving her an allowance; taking her money; not letting her know about or have access to family income.

USING EMOTIONAL ABUSE: Putting her down; making her feel bad about herself; calling her names; making her think she's crazy; playing mind games; humiliating her; making her feel guilty.

POWER AND CONTROL

USING MALE PRIVILEGE: Treating her like a servant; making all the big decisions; acting the 'master of the castle'; being the one to define men's and women's roles.

USING ISOLATION: Controlling what she does, who she sees and talks to, what she reads, where she goes; limiting her outside involvement; using jealousy to justify actions.

USING CHILDREN: Making her feel guilty about the children; using the children to relay messages; using visitation to harass her; threatening to take the children away.

MINIMIZING, DENYING AND BLAMING: Making light of the abuse and not taking her concerns about it seriously; saying the abuse didn't happen; shifting responsibility for abusive behaviour; saying she caused it.

The Duluth Wheel

Economic abuse

Hillary married a middle-aged businessman who, until their marriage, had always lived with his mother. After the wedding, Hillary and her teenage son moved in with them both, in accommodation above the business, which was a busy general store. Hillary was soon expected to help in the business—in effect, it was run by her. She worked long hours in the shop, which they opened early to deal with the morning papers and kept open until late evening to benefit from the off-licence trade. When she was not at the counter she was expected to do the accounts and stock ordering. Her husband refused to pay her for any of her work. She was not even given any pocket money. Her husband claimed that her working in his business merely paid for the food and board she used in the home. Holidays were not permitted as it cost the husband to keep her while she was not working. When she was first married, Hillary used her small savings to pay for food and for the household bills, which her husband would just ignore until the bailiffs arrived or the gas was cut off. Eventually the money ran out. Her mother-in-law would shop for her husband's food but would refuse to allow Hillary and her son to eat from their cupboard. For a long time Hillary ate only cereals or the food from the shop which had passed its sell-by date. Her son survived on his school dinners and the scraps she could take out of the shop for him. She lost a tremendous amount of weight and was forced to dress in clothing from charity shops. Hillary endured this situation for three years before persuading the authorities that she was living separately from her husband—although under the same roof—and so qualified for income support.

Other abusers may similarly keep a partner short of money, perhaps preventing her working, or taking child allowance from her. Or they may take family savings which were intended for something special—perhaps a holiday or a child's present—and blow them all on drink or gambling without the victim knowing. One surprisingly common (and particularly degrading) form of economic abuse is a man refusing to give his partner money for sanitary protection. This ensures that the woman is humiliated and effectively confined to the house for a time each month. In other cases the abuse is more subtle.

Shirley found that when she and Dave set up home together he expected her to look after the household finances and to take responsibility for making sure she went to the bank or post office to pay the bills. At first she didn't mind this—she enjoyed doing the household accounts and, since she was not working, it was more convenient for her to attend to it than for Dave to do so. However, after a while Dave stopped giving her all his wages. He would keep some or, on occasion, all of it from her. The bills were in his name and, since she was not allowed to open his post, he sometimes kept the bills from her until she had missed the time for payment. Inevitably she fell behind with her payments and Dave started to use this as a cause for arguments and eventually violence. He would tell her that she ought to plan ahead and not rely on his weekly wage packet. He did not want her to work but at the same time told her that since he was the one working he was entitled to some of his wages. Shirley was actually very sensible with money and it was only when she found herself contemplating taking a loan from a loan shark that she realized she could not live with the situation any longer.

Keeping a woman short of money disempowers her. It may well mean that she has to approach her partner for money every time she needs something, which gives him the opportunity to judge her or criticize her for her needs or desires. It takes away the victim's ability to do things by herself without her partner's knowledge. Lack of money may prevent her leaving the home or seeking help. She may feel that she cannot afford to leave with no access to resources of her own to start again. Or, more simply, a woman who lives in an isolated area may need a bus fare to get to see a solicitor or a citizens' help group. Further, without money to spend on social activities, it is easy for a woman to become isolated which is in itself another form of domestic abuse.

Isolation

An abuser may use a number of tactics to isolate his victim from friends, family or other sources of support:

He may listen in to all her telephone conversations and read her mail.

He may refuse to let her go out alone to visit family or to socialize with friends.

He may behave so badly in front of her friends and family that they cease to visit her at home.

He may force her to move house often, thus preventing her from being near her family or from building up friendships near her home.

Even where the parties do not live together the abuser can create isolation.

Pat had been separated from her husband for three years. She left him because of his violence and dishonesty. However, they remained legally married and he would come round to her new home and threaten or use violence on her. This became more frequent after she started a new relationship and he found out about it. He started to spy on her and to use violence both in public places and in the home, saying it was his 'right'—she was his wife. She sought legal advice after he broke her wrist. She said:

I'm frightened to go out in case he sees me. Even when I was coming here on the bus, I thought I saw his car and I was scared. I have to keep my curtains drawn in the day so he can't see what I am doing in the house. My friends—this sounds daft but it's true—have a special code for knocking on my door so I know to open it to them. I just want to be able to go out again.

The effect of the isolation is to remove the abuser's perceived causes of jealousy. If his partner never leaves the house she cannot be having an affair. If she is never able to see her girlfriends they cannot be persuading her to act against his wishes. It also means she is more able to concentrate on the abuser's needs and demands. Without outside interests her whole world will become focused on her home. She can never be too busy to cook his tea or clean the house for him.

The effect of isolation is particularly pernicious when combined with emotional abuse. If an abuser is constantly telling a woman she is no good and that the violence is her fault, she will have nobody else to tell her otherwise if she is in isolation. In this way the effects of the abuser's words are increased because the victim receives no balancing opinions. She may compare herself to the other people she can see through the windows of her living room. She may begin to believe that something must be wrong with her. After all, her neighbours seem to cope with life much better than she does.

By the use of isolating tactics an abuser can even con outsiders into thinking that his partner must be the problem. A common habit of abusers is for them to time their partners doing an everyday task. For example, a man may calculate that it takes his partner ten minutes to walk to the school, collect the children and bring them home. She is then allowed precisely ten minutes every day—no more, no less. A minute late and she faces recriminations. She may well be accused of meeting another man while she is out. The effect of this is that she will be reluctant to stop and chat with other mothers or with staff at the school for fear of violence on her return. Playground gossip may then brand her stuck-up or snooty. Other mothers will not understand why she will not stop to talk to them and will give up trying to befriend her. Teachers may ask her to hold on for five minutes to discuss her child's progress. When she refuses they may believe her to be uninterested in her child's education. Suddenly the woman is the problem. It is all down to her personality.

Crucially, a victim in isolation will often find it harder to leave an abuser. She will have no friends to give her moral support or offers of alternative accommodation. She will have no one to confide in who will give her moral support and emotional strength. She may not be aware of the existence of support groups or other sources of help. If she is, she may not be able to access them without the abuser finding out and retaliating.

Using intimidation

Abusers can often control their victims by intimidation. This can take various forms.

One abuser would clean his gun in front of his wife. When challenged about it he would say he was only maintaining it—just like she emptied the Hoover. However, it was done in such a manner as to leave his wife in no doubt that he was showing her he had a gun which he would use against her if he felt he needed to.

Another man would smash up furniture and break personal items of the victim as an indication that she could be next.

A third man was a six-foot-one rugby player. His wife, who was not particularly tall to begin with, was always forced to be seated during their arguments. He towered above her, blocking her path.

Sometimes intimidation on its own can be just as effective as the violence itself. This is particularly so when there has been a pattern of past violence. As one victim said:

He would simply stand in front of me and put his right hand on the buckle of his belt. No more, no less. But I would do what he said because I knew that what he meant was that if I didn't obey him he would just take the belt off and beat me with it. He'd done it enough before for me to know he would do it again.

The hidden agenda which can exist behind so many gestures of this kind means that an abuser can use intimidation to control a victim in public without anyone else realizing what he is doing. The victim will be able to pick up subtle signs from her partner which will go unnoticed by others in a room.

Coercion and threats

Closely linked to intimidation is an abuser's use of coercion and threats. These may be threats of physical violence:

'If you leave I'll find you and kill you.'

'If you chat up that shopkeeper again I will break your legs.'

'If you don't come to bed I will just force you.'

Or it may be threats to do something else, designed to make her fall in with his plans:

'If you divorce me I'll kill myself.'

'If you go telling your mother our private business again I'll really give her something to worry about.'

'If you phone the police I'll tell them that it was you who hit the children.'

Threats such as this make the victims choose between actual violence or colluding with the abuser to keep the violence a secret. The result can be that a victim feels she has actually played a part in condoning that violence by not standing up to it, even though the alternative may be to risk even worse abuse.

Women can later feel stupid or guilty for not seeking help when in fact it was the abuse itself which prevented them from doing so.

Abusers may coerce victims into activities which will compromise them. The abuser can then hold this against them. This may involve criminal activity. A woman may be kept short of money and be forced to shoplift to feed her family. Where the man is involved in criminal activities it is not unusual for him to involve his partner. He may force her to hide stolen goods or to pass drugs. In this way she becomes further enmeshed in his life. She may be afraid to complain to the police about his violence for fear that she will be found out. Knowing she has participated in activities which she may well despise also demoralizes her and contributes to the destruction of her sense of self-worth. This in itself makes her more vulnerable to violence and less able to seek help.

Emotional abuse

Emotional abuse is one of the most common and most destructive aspects of domestic violence. Often it accompanies other forms of abuse and pervades the whole of a victim's life. It can include any of the following.

Name-calling
The phrase 'Sticks and stones may break my bones but names can never hurt me' is simply not true in the context of domestic violence. Calling a person names dehumanizes them and turns them more into an object than a character with their own identity. Many of the derogatory terms used for women are sexual in nature—'slag', 'whore', 'slut' and worse. Their constant use powerfully reflects the abuser's view of the woman's role and worth.

Constant criticism

Mandy said:

Everything I did was wrong. I was stupid and slow. I was greedy and scheming. I was lazy. For a long time I believed him. I thought I deserved it when he hit me. I thought that there was no point in me leaving—I would never manage without him, and there was certainly no way I would find anyone else. It was only when he put me into hospital that I got talking to a nurse who was so kind to me. I thought, if I am so useless then he won't miss me and at least I will be safe. So I left him.

The criticism may be made to others and be calculated to gain the abuser credibility and sympathy. Regular stories about the victim—'She had another tantrum last night, like a child', 'I have to dress the kids myself before I go to work, otherwise she won't do it'—can have a gradual effect. Without anyone being aware of it the abuser can paint a picture of himself as the hard-done-by one in the relationship. Then, if the victim tells about the violence, she is either less likely to be believed or else it will be assumed that she pushed her partner to the end of his tether and 'drove him to it'.

Casting doubts on the victim's sanity

One abuser took his wife to the doctors. Terrified to say anything, she sat there while her husband showed the doctor the wounds he had inflicted—which clearly needed treatment. He explained how she was self-mutilating and would lie irrationally. He wanted psychiatric treatment for her.

Other cases are less extreme, but the abuser may on a regular basis tell the victim that she is imagining the abuse or that people will think her mad if she accuses her seemingly respectable husband of abusing her. Repeated enough times to an already distressed and traumatized victim, these thoughts will begin to take root in her own mind, causing her great anguish and torment. Many abusers are capable of presenting a completely different personality to those outside the home. When the woman sees this side of him it is easy to wonder whether that is his true persona and the violent man is just her imagination. Because no one else sees the violence, she has no one to back her up and his accusations begin to make sense.

Using the children

Emotional abuse can also involve the abuser using the children as a tactic to upset the victim. He may seek to prevent her leaving by telling her how much the children will suffer. He may tell her that she is a bad mother for breaking up the family. An abuser may threaten to harm the children:

Chris was asked for sex by her partner one night. She refused and he gave her a choice. Either she went upstairs with him or he would force her—in front of the children.

Shelly had a two-month-old daughter by her boyfriend. He smashed all the furniture in the flat and threatened that if she ever sought help for his violent behaviour he would take the baby abroad without her.

Where the parties have separated it is not uncommon for the abuser to try and use the children to 'persuade' the victim to return.

Cindy eventually left her abusive husband, taking her five-year-old daughter Laura with her. Her two sons stayed with their father. Cindy believed that it was her husband's poisoning of the two boys' minds that lay behind their refusal to see her.

The last time I spoke to Karl on the phone he called me a slut. He said that I'd made his dad unhappy and I was wrong to leave him. But he saw all the violence—he saw him hit me. Laura wants to see her dad, and I'd never stop them, but he's trying it on her too. She asked me the other night, after seeing him, why I was a bad mummy. Then she started to cry. I asked her what was wrong, but she said that daddy would be cross if she told me. I promised not to tell and she told me that her dad had said she would be better living with him in case I left her alone too. Every time she comes home from contact with her dad I find notes from him hidden in her pockets or her bag. They are usually threats to me. Last time it was a family photo with my face cut out.

Using male privilege

In many abusive relationships the atmosphere is one of the male being in absolute control—the boss. Apart from the violent and abusive behaviour which reinforces the abuser's control, there may be other ways in which his authority is reinforced within the family:

He is the breadwinner and works. He will not help with housework or childcare. That is 'women's work'.

He handles all the financial decisions—she is given a small allowance for housekeeping, for which she must account. All money is in his name—she has no chequebook or credit cards to use.

He makes the decisions—which schools the children attend, where the family go on holiday, or whether they move house.

He insists that he should be the only one to drive the family car.

In other words, the relationship is run on the basis of gender stereotyping. This runs beyond the agreed division of responsibilities between the partners. It means the woman is dependent on her husband and her life is lived according to his whims. It denies her the right to be her own person, with views and wishes of her own. Suppressing a woman's very humanity can be just as abusive as a physical beating.

Minimizing, denying and blaming

The tactics of minimizing, denying and blaming underlie and reinforce other abusive behaviour. They reflect an abuser's inability—or refusal—to acknowledge the nature and effects of his behaviour. He may seek to minimize the violence to his partner:

'Oh what are you crying for—it was only a love tap.'
'Everyone loses his temper now and again. It's not that big a deal. No one else would make such a fuss.'

Or he may seek to minimize it to third parties, such as the police or a solicitor:

'She is exaggerating. OK, I pushed her, but I didn't ever hit her.'
'That bruise looks worse than it is. She bruises easily.'

Or he may deny his behaviour completely:

'She's lying just to get me out of the house.'
'It wasn't deliberate at all—she tripped and fell down the stairs, and she knows it.'

Abusers frequently seek to pass the responsibility for their actions on to something or someone else:

'She provoked me.'
'I was drunk. It wasn't really my fault.'
'Everyone else hits their wives — I don't want to look soft in front of my mates. They all saw her smiling at that barman.'

These tactics are useful in allowing an abuser to believe that his behaviour is justified and can therefore continue. They have a debilitating effect on the victim, however. She may be left wondering whether she is overreacting or imagining things. Or she may feel that she is at fault and, therefore, cannot take action against the abuser. His refusal to acknowledge his behaviour also removes from her any hope that he may recognize their problem and work with her to repair their relationship.

Domestic violence is not confined to isolated incidents of physical abuse. It is about a way of life—a course of treatment of a victim. The types of domestic violence mentioned above blur together in a complex web of violence, control and domination in which the victim becomes ensnared. If you are suffering in any of the ways talked about above then there are some important points for you to remember:

Domestic violence is about power and control of a victim. It is not a joke—it is serious and victims should never feel ashamed about seeking help.

There are various different ways in which you can get help if you are suffering from domestic violence and this book will talk about many of them. You should know that people will help you even if you wish to stay in the relationship. It doesn't matter if you have asked for help before—many women need help several times in their lives.

You could be a victim of domestic violence without ever actually being hit. If you are in a relationship where the abuse is non-physical, help is still available for you.

Domestic violence can happen to anyone anywhere. It occurs across age, race, class and gender. Although it may seem like it, you are not the only woman with this problem, as the next chapter shows.

CHAPTER 2

A lone cry?

As a solicitor I can see several women a week who are suffering from domestic violence in one way or another. All those women are different and yet they all tend to have at least one thing in common—they feel alone. Seeking legal help can be daunting—no woman relishes the prospect of telling a stranger about her most intimate secrets and fears. However, once women begin talking to me they are able to go beyond the bare facts of their situation and are often able to express how they feel about the situation. Many emotions come out during our discussions—fear, anger, disappointment, surprise, bitterness, desperation, bewilderment, despair, shame, worry, determination to improve their situation and so on. Depending on their personality and individual situation, each woman will experience different emotions at different stages of her experience, many of which are shared with other victims.

However, almost every woman who comes into my office talks about how she feels alone in one way or another. One woman, Kerry, a young mother in her twenties whose husband was a carpet layer, kept asking me whether I believed her. She would tell me part of the story and then apologize, 'I know it sounds stupid but he really did do it.'

She had been quite badly assaulted, but was keen for reassurance.

'The courts will believe me, won't they?—it sounds just like a soap-opera story, but it's true.'

After a little while I stopped making notes of what she was telling me and started to talk to her, instead of just listening. I told her that as a firm we often took several women like her to court each week, and that other solicitors in the town did the same. I told her about the local Women's Aid group who did nothing but help victims of domestic violence day in, day out. She stared at me, amazed, and then—for the first time since she had entered my office—she smiled.

'I had no idea,' she said. 'I thought I was the only one this had ever happened to.'

Other women know about domestic violence, but feel that they are the only one in their social circle who can ever have experienced the problem. I once acted for a woman who was an accountant. Her husband was a self-employed businessman and they lived in the 'good part of town'. She told me about the injuries her husband had caused her and then added, 'You always think it happens to someone else, don't you? Not in families like mine.'

I was able to reassure her that I had acted for other women in similar jobs and income brackets to her, and she drew some comfort from this.

'It makes me feel less of a freak,' she said. 'I thought you would think me odd—that you wouldn't expect someone like me to need your help.'

Many victims feel like these women—that they are alone in their suffering and that no one else knows what they are going through. The old adage 'A problem shared is a problem halved' does hold some truth. Suffering can be made worse by a sense of isolation. As human beings we naturally seek solace, comfort and strength in shared experience. Courage can be found in numbers and often victims find the will to change their situations in the support of others. In fact, as we will see, domestic violence is a widespread problem. So, why do so many victims start by feeling that their complaints are a lone cry?

Abuser's behaviour

In Chapter 1 we saw that isolation can in itself be an element of the domestic violence. It may be that the abuser deliberately keeps the victim away from sources of support and understanding. He may, in the process of emotionally abusing the woman, tell her that no one will believe her complaints and that she is the only woman who would ever complain of his behaviour. Comments like this, coming as they so often do from an abuser who holds an enormous amount of power over the victim, can have a strong effect. For a victim who hears this kind of message from her abuser it is important to remember that not everything the abuser says is true. It may be a deliberate attempt to intimidate the victim and to prevent her from getting help, or from involving the police to the detriment of the abuser.

Having said that, a woman who has believed what the abuser says should not feel stupid for having done so. It is a natural consequence of the violence, constant emotional abuse and the power imbalance in the relationship that she will give at least some credence to what the abuser says.

Victim's own feelings

It is not unusual for victims to turn inward when seeking to find reasons for the violence. The next chapter looks at some of the reasons the violence may happen and stresses that it is not the victim's fault. That is easier to see when, like myself, you have had the chance to read about the topic and talk to people who work in the field, and when you have not suffered violence yourself. When you are still trapped in the violent relationship, it is not always that clear.

Many women feel shame at what has happened to them. They feel unable to speak about it or to ask for help. This is especially so if the violence has a sexual element to it. They may feel guilty and be reluctant to seek support, for fear of being rejected or blamed for putting themselves in their situation.

Many women who speak to me express the view that they are at fault for going into the relationship in the first place. Mandy spoke for a lot of women when she said to me, 'I knew he'd been violent in the past but I thought it would all change when I married him. I thought it would be different then. I was so stupid.'

Another client thought her childhood experiences should have taught her to choose her partners more carefully.

'My mother put up with this for five years from my father. I know they say you always pick boyfriends like your father, but you'd think I'd have known better, wouldn't you?'

Other women feel that they may be at fault for starting off the violence in the first place. Women ask me such things as, 'It is not unreasonable of me to be angry when he drinks away the children's school dinner money, is it?' or 'The courts won't think it was my fault because I went out to bingo that night, will they? After all, if he'd been able to go out instead of having to babysit perhaps he wouldn't have got so angry.'

Again, the next chapter shows that just because some women have these kinds of needs and expectations, that is not a justification for their partners to be violent to them. Nevertheless, it is not unnatural for women to make these kinds of assumptions. Women who are still at the stage of believing that they are at fault may feel too guilty or too stupid to seek help.

Often it is only when the woman begins to speak about her situation that she finds out there are others in her position. If she speaks to a solicitor she will be told that laws exist to protect her because the situation is a common one. If she speaks to a help group she will meet women who share her experience. If she confides in her doctor he or she may assure her that she is not alone. However, until she is able to take that step, many women labour under the misapprehension that they are alone in their predicament.

If you are feeling that way, remember that the reason for the violence may be more complex than you think. The next chapter may help you understand this.

It is natural for you to feel alone but that can change. The rest of this book will give you ideas about the kind of support you can get and shows you that other people will not reject you for being a victim.

Social attitudes

Some women may feel isolated because of the pressures society places on them. Perhaps you are a member of a cultural minority whose community places great emphasis on the privacy of family matters. Perhaps you feel that you cannot break out of the relationship because of community pressure. Again—you are not alone. The Newham Asian Women's Project annual report 1993/4 tells the story of Shantiben:

> Shantiben had suffered domestic violence for most of her 30-year marriage. Her strict religious background prevented her having any thoughts of leaving her husband, as did the pressures from friends and family to 'make it work' even after her two children had grown up and left home. During one severe beating her husband threw her out. She came into our refuge feeling very afraid but also ashamed that she had left home. Once she saw that she was not alone, that there were other women in similar circumstances who did not judge her but helped and supported her, she began the process of rebuilding her life. Her children, happy that their mother had finally left home, were extremely supportive. She was eventually temporarily rehoused by the local authority, but has also been offered a self-contained flat in the Hamara Ghar project where she will not feel isolated. Shantiben has now settled into a happy and independent lifestyle.

This story also illustrates how religious pressure may make a victim feel isolated. Perhaps a church or other religious community places great store by the woman's submission to a man. It is easy for a woman to feel that unless she puts up with the violence she will be rejected by her religion.

Other women may have made an attempt to share their plight with someone else and have encountered a less than sympathetic response. Obviously, if a woman's story is not sympathetically received the first time, it becomes more difficult to make further attempts to seek help. Domestic violence is beginning to get more publicity as women's groups seek to educate people. Soap operas, such as 'Brookside' and 'Coronation Street', have written it into their storylines, which has caused people to talk more about the issue.

Nevertheless, not everyone will understand the complexity of the victim's situation. Friends and family may just not understand how a victim can stay with a violent man. They may be embarrassed to talk about the subject with a victim. They may even be silent victims themselves, who are reluctant to talk about the issue since they are not yet ready to reveal their own experiences. Also, if they are close to the abuser, they may feel split loyalties or be afraid to help the victim for fear of retribution from the abuser. All these things may be reasons why the victim feels alone and misunderstood.

If you have experienced these attitudes from other people it may help you to know that the people you have turned to may not be able to help you because of their own experiences—or lack of them. However, there *are* people who will understand and accept your story. This book goes on to explain the type of support available to you and the appendices give you some addresses and telephone numbers of people who will accept you and listen to your story.

How widespread is domestic violence?

How big a problem is domestic violence then? Is it just something which only happens to a few women a year? Is it a problem which is exaggerated by the feminists who wish to put men down? Is it hyped up by the media?

It is difficult to get exact figures of the number of women who suffer from domestic violence. Not all incidents are reported to the police, and so figures based on their statistics are an underestimate. Even so, the figures which are available show an alarmingly high rate of domestic violence in this country—especially if the figures are not complete. The following sample statistics show how big a problem it really is.

A study from Middlesex University showed that:

As many as 1 in 10 women were victims of domestic violence.

1 in 17 women were forced to have sex with their partners without consent.

1 in 5 men struck their partners.

6 in 10 men saw violence against their partners as an option in the future.[1]

A sample of 1,007 married women were asked to take place in a survey in the street during August and September 1989. Of the women who were interviewed, a third said that they had experienced violence in their marriage. Of those in the survey who were now divorced or separated, 59% had been hit by their husbands.[2]

The British Crime Survey in 1992 estimated that half of all offences of violence against women involved domestic violence. The same survey estimated that only one fifth of all incidents of domestic violence are reported to the police, and that domestic violence is as common an occurrence for women aged 16-29 as pub-related violence is for men of the same age group.

Questionnaires filled in anonymously by women in hospital emergency departments showed that 24-35% had experienced domestic violence.[3]

Of women divorcing their husbands, 70% cite violence as one of the reasons for the breakdown of the marriage.

What kind of people does domestic violence affect?

Domestic violence is no respecter of persons. It can happen to anyone anywhere of any age, class, race or occupation. If asked to describe the type of woman who is a victim of domestic violence, many people would say it is the mother struggling on income support in poor housing with an unemployed husband. Women in this predicament do suffer. However, the spectrum is much wider than that. Women in all walks of life can suffer from domestic violence:

Hannah was a 72-year-old retired nursing manager who had been abused all her married life.

Kath was a 44-year-old with an admitted alcohol problem. She was unemployed, being unable to keep a job down. Despite her continual requests, her violent cohabitee refused to leave the council house which was in her sole name.

Carole was a wealthy wife of a company director, resident in a smart village with a nanny to look after her children.

Shelly was a seventeen-year-old single mother of two, who lived alone in a damp council flat. Her ex-boyfriend would not leave her alone. Despite her predicament, she was too young to get legal aid on her own account and had to apply via a friend who was over eighteen.

Debbie was a mother of two in her thirties. She and her husband—who worked in the local glass factory—owned a small terraced house. She encouraged the children to take part in the activities of the local church and took pride in running their home on a modest budget. Their marriage ran into difficulties when her husband lost affection for her and started to stay away from the home. It was only once she started to seek legal advice that he assaulted her.

Mary was a psychiatric nurse, married to a businessman who earned a good salary in his career as a management consultant. She became over-friendly with one patient she met and let it develop into an affair. She realized her mistake and tried to end it for the sake of her marriage, but he refused to let her go and began to stalk her and spy on her family. She was forced to pay privately to obtain an injunction against him.

The catchment areas of the offices in which I have worked have not had a high percentage of ethnic minorities in the population. However, it is clear that domestic violence is not just confined to the white, middle-class, Christian section of our population. Recently, a Jewish women's helpline has been set up to assist Jewish victims of violence. In the Toxteth area of Liverpool there is a refuge providing for women of ethnic minorities. Part of their facilities provides especially for the needs of Muslim women. There are other projects around the country—such as the Newham Asian Women's Project or Southhall Black Sisters—who have found that the incidence of violence within the ethnic minority communities justifies specific provision for these women.

Nor is the problem limited to heterosexual relationships. Couples within the gay community have also experienced domestic violence. Indeed, the gay activist group Stonewall has been campaigning for some time for the domestic violence legislation to be widened to apply to homosexual relationships also.

Can men be victims of domestic violence?

For a long time no one actually believed that men could be victims of domestic violence. The emphasis is still on women as the victims, but it is becoming more clear that men can be victims too. Journalist Victoria Freedman wrote an article in the *Irish Times* in 1995 quoting a man called Les Davidson who had, in 1994, set up a helpline in Britain for male victims. He told her:

It is happening right across the board, from builders to doctors. Such things as premenstrual syndrome and post-natal depression have been identified as possibly making women aggressive. Or, in the same way that men are aggressive, it could be as a result of family life, role models, the concealment of abuse or stress at work...

I was, and still am, appalled by what men do to women. But a few years ago I began to get calls from men too. I know it's hard to believe. Society has given men a role in which they are not acknowledged as victims. If a woman slaps a man, society gives her an excuse for her actions. But should a man slap a woman he is a batterer...

Most injuries to men are to the back of the shoulder, with women using mainly kitchen weapons such as knives and scissors. Hot liquid is poured onto the lap. There are a lot of attacks to the genital area...

The pattern of abuse involves control and removing your partner's self-esteem. Everybody has the ability to do that, men and women. I now see domestic violence as a social issue, not as a gender issue.

In 1995 Audrey Macklin completed a PhD thesis at Liverpool John Moores University, entitled 'Battered Husbands: The Hidden Victims'. She interviewed a number of male victims from various walks of life—including a student, a milkman, a chef, a policeman, a pilot, a religious leader, a retired schoolteacher and an unemployed man. They described their experiences of being abused in various ways:

I've had loads of black eyes because she's punched me with her fist as well as smacking me in the eye with her shoe, once she even smacked me in the eye with a pair of edging shears... I had to have seven stitches.

The physical abuse was not as bad as the emotional and psychological abuse, I don't think so anyway. The physical injuries heal but I live with the pain of the other abuse every day.

When my wife goes berserk she is like an unknown demented creature. Although she had physically abused and tortured me, the worst time was when she locked me out after I had gone to hospital because she had pushed me down the stairs. She changed the locks straight away and told her family I was having an affair. It was awful. I didn't see the kids for a couple of months that time, but I did go to the school several times to see them and talk to them when they had finished. Have you any idea what it's like to miss your kids, to miss saying goodnight to them or wishing them a good day at school? Let me tell you, the pain is unbearable.

I was the one with the black eyes, the scratched face, at times even the knife wounds—the list of injuries is endless, but it never stopped. Oh yes, I mean the beatings stopped for a week if I was lucky, but because I never knew when she would have a tantrum or fit of aggression it was like living in a bubble. I was petrified in case I said something or didn't do something, afraid to do things or frightened in case I forgot to do something. Living like this makes you paranoid you know, you question your own mental state and sometimes even believe that it is your own fault, but you don't know how it can be your fault.

For a long time, society has not recognized that men can be

victims of domestic violence. It is not clear why this is, but several reasons can be suggested.

It may have a lot to do with the fact that much of the research and action on domestic violence has come from a feminist standpoint. The emphasis placed on men's systematic power over women has not made it easy to fit male victims into the picture. It is assumed that women, because of their size and strength, are not capable of inflicting violence on men. However, as Audrey Macklin points out, this does not take into account the fact that the man is not always the strongest partner—ill health or old age can alter physique. No strength is needed to inflict psychological damage. Also, weapon use makes up for physical strength.

Also, it may be that male victims have not been as willing as female victims to come forward and admit their problem. It may be that society finds it easier to accept women as weak victims needing help. Since men are portrayed as macho, self-providing creatures, it may be doubly hard for men to admit they are victims—they have an extra hurdle to overcome.

It may be, too, that men are in a better position to help themselves. Even a man who is a victim is likely to be in a stronger position than a woman when it comes to being able to leave the home. He is less likely to be tied down by childcare requirements and more likely to be able to work to pay for alternative accommodation.

The other side to the argument is that fewer men come forward because there are fewer services available to them. This is partly because the problem is not recognized as being worthy of either consideration or financial support. A social-work team leader interviewed by Audrey Macklin said:

> It is not a recognized problem within society; men are never seen as the victim in these situations, only women. Because we are financially restricted, obviously resources are geared towards the recognised problem: women as victims of domestic violence.

The victims who participated in the survey had wanted help and found it unavailable. As one said:

I've tried the police, the social services, and FNF [Families Need Fathers]. You'd be surprised where and who I have tried, all to no avail, which has just added to my frustration.

I personally accept that men can be victims of domestic violence and are just as deserving as women of help and support. Throughout the book I have referred to the victim as the female and the perpetrator as male. There are two reasons for this. Firstly, to refer to both genders throughout would be cumbersome. The introduction makes it clear that the genders should be read as interchangeable where appropriate. Secondly, men are only just beginning to be acknowledged as victims. This means that most of the information and research available refers only to women. Equivalent statistics and theories are simply not available for male victims. I sincerely hope that this will change in the near future and that I will have to update this book to reflect the new research. The book is, therefore, written primarily on the basis that the victim is female, but with a clear acknowledgment that the roles can be reversed and men should not be excluded.

1. From 'The Hidden Figures: Domestic Violence in North London', Middlesex University Centre for Criminology.
2. Kate Painter, 'Wife Rape in the UK', a paper presented to the American Society of Criminology 1991, San Francisco.
3. 'Domestic Violence', the report of a national interagency working party, Victim Support, 1992.

CHAPTER 3

Why is this happening to me?

Domestic violence is a bewildering experience. A victim will not have expected violence when the relationship began. They will have started a life with their partner full of hope and trust in him. When the assaults and the abuse begin many victims will ask themselves, What went wrong? Why has he started to hit me? Anne suffered domestic violence for seven years and would torment herself with these questions.

Every time he had hit me I would rack my brains trying to understand—why me? I thought that if I could only work out why he did it to me then perhaps I could understand how to stop it. Sometimes I thought it would be something obvious—because I had burned his toast or because my mother—whom he hated—had been round to see me. But at other times there seemed to be no possible reason—no explanation at all. I so badly wanted there to be a reason—any reason. If it was all without a reason then there was no hope at all. I would try to come up with possible excuses for his behaviour, no matter how illogical they were. At first that was helpful. I would make an excuse for him and, as long as I didn't think about it too closely, I could cope with the violence. Eventually, however, I had to acknowledge that none of the excuses rang true in my heart. I just didn't know why he did it. If I didn't know, there was no chance I could do anything about it. It was when I finally admitted that, that I first sought help.

Many victims search for a reason for the violence. Some, like Anne, believe a reason is the first step to finding a solution. Others may just want an explanation as an antidote to the raging feelings of injustice they experience. They may have friends or relatives who have loving and caring relationships. They may want to know why they cannot have what their acquaintances have. Why are they different? Victims who have religious beliefs may struggle to understand how their God could let this happen to them. Is it really part of what is planned for them, or is everything going terribly wrong? If so, why doesn't their God rescue them?

It is not easy to come up with a simple answer to that question. However, there are many different theories about social causes and many beliefs that victims hold which are useful to look at.

Is it the victim's fault?

Many victims assume that the violence is their own fault. They think that their abuser is angered by something they have done. Or perhaps they simply deserve no better because they are such a worthless person. They may think to themselves such things as:

'If only I could get the house tidy and the children in bed before he came home he wouldn't be so irritated.'

'If I could only learn to say the right thing then he wouldn't get so annoyed with me.'

'If only I wasn't so stupid he wouldn't despise me so much.'

'If only he had been my first husband he wouldn't feel so insecure about me.'

These beliefs are often backed up by what the abuser may say to his partner. Physical violence is, as we have seen, often accompanied by verbal abuse. Part of that abuse may be the abuser trying to place the blame for his actions on the victim. He may seek to excuse his behaviour by criticizing his victim.

He may well say that he is only violent because she is such a bad housekeeper he cannot help but be angry with her. Or he may say that he just gets so frustrated because she cannot ever seem to manage on the small amount of housekeeping he gives her—she is just greedy, and cannot understand that after a hard day at work his drinking money is as important as the children's school uniforms.

However, many women find that on a closer look they are blamed for things that they have not done or for things which are not their fault. For example, an abuser may blame the woman for failing to make sure that there was sufficient milk for his breakfast. However, it may be that that particular morning the milkman was later than usual. Or perhaps the abuser was angry because the victim failed to keep the baby quiet while the football was on television. However, the baby may be teething and refuse to stop crying. The abuser may even make contradictory demands from his partner so that she cannot win. Anne found this:

One night he asked me to go to the pub with him. I was sitting in a group of friends—there was another woman there but the rest were his mates from work. I was actually having a good time—there was lots of laughing and joking and I joined in with it all. When I got home he began to slap me around, saying that he would not stand for me flirting with the men and trying to be the centre of attention. I avoided going to the pub with him for a few days but the next Friday was our neighbour's birthday and he insisted I go with him to celebrate. I went, but I was careful to sit in the corner and avoided speaking wherever possible. When we got home he hit me again, saying he was ashamed to have such a miserable wife and that I deliberately showed him up.

It may be that in a small number of families the parties do have genuine 'fights' where each partner provokes the other into a mutual display of violence. However, this is not the same as incidents of domestic violence where there is an imbalance of power and one partner is deliberately and systematically abusing the other. Attempting to blame the victim is usually just the abuser seeking to avoid responsibility for his own actions and is, in itself, a form of abuse.

It may well be that an individual act of violence is sparked off by the victim doing something small to annoy her abuser. Perhaps she has spilled tea on the new carpet, or perhaps she forgot to pick his suit up from the cleaners. Even in those cases, it is important to remember that no one has the right to 'punish' their partner by physical assault. Everyone makes mistakes or annoys another person at some time. This is not a justification for them to use violence against you. Domestic violence is wrong. It is the fault of the abuser, not the victim.

Is it all down to alcohol?

Victims and abusers alike often associate overuse of alcohol with domestic violence. There is no doubt that there is often an association. A study in the British Medical Journal found that of 100 abusers 74 had a drinking problem. Other, mainly American, research studies show that between 36 and 52% of wife-batterers also abused alcohol.

Indeed, the Bible recognizes that alcohol can adversely influence behaviour.

'Wine is a mocker and beer a brawler; whoever is led astray by them is not wise' (Proverbs 20:1).

However, it is over-simplistic to say that alcohol is the cause of domestic violence. Sometimes it can simply be a convenient excuse for the abuser. He can beat his wife and claim, 'It wasn't really me—it was the drink. I wouldn't have done it if I hadn't had a pint or two.'

Often this is not true. A man who has a drink problem may beat his wife even when he is not under the influence of alcohol. The drink could just be something which loosens inhibitions and makes it easier for an abuser to act on underlying violent tendencies. He may often want to hit his wife, but manages to hold back because he is afraid the children may see him. After a drink, his judgment may be clouded and he may not see that as a reason for holding back. Or the drink may fill him with bravado which he doesn't usually possess.

'I will do what I like to my wife—stuff the kids. They'll just have to get used to it.'

Even where the alcohol is closely associated with the violence, the abuser's drinking habits may be symptoms of the same problems which cause the violence in the first place. Tracy's husband was a high wage earner until the recession hit and he was made redundant. He began to drink and to hit her.

At first I blamed the drinking. Only after counselling did I realize that it was more to do with his inability to handle his redundancy. He used to pour out all his frustrations and disappointments on me—with his fists. The drinking was just a cover for his own shame.

What about all the violence in society as a whole?

It is possible that some abusers use violence because the society in which they live not only condones the violence but encourages men to be violent. Men who kill in war are rewarded by being made heroes and presented with medals. Action films portray the hero of the action as the man who can kill, fight and cause destruction. The peaceful option is not so manly. Most men would prefer to be compared to Arnold Schwarzenegger or Sylvester Stallone than Gandhi or Archbishop Desmond Tutu.

The same applies in sport. Men are more likely to wish to emulate boxer Frank Bruno or rugby-league player V'ainga Tuigamala than ice dancer Christopher Dean.

Male children are brought up with violent role models. Generally they are bought toy guns rather than play kitchens, toys such as Action Man or Power Rangers rather than Barbie dolls or My Little Pony.

A male child involved in playground skirmishes is more likely than a girl to be told to fight back—to stand up for himself. For a girl to 'scrap' is unladylike. For a boy to resist is for him to be considered weak and a 'sissy'.

It may be that violence becomes a learned behaviour, that men are so conditioned into being tough and physical that this trickles over into the family. Men in general still do not find it as easy as women to express their emotions freely. Many may find it hard to negotiate a compromise in a relationship since this will involve discussion about personal issues. When faced with a confrontation their instinct will be to fight for their own viewpoint, as they have been taught.

It is also possible that constant exposure to violent forms of entertainment, violent sports and even graphic portrayals of war on television cause observers to be desensitized—the violence no longer shocks and is increasingly seen as acceptable. For example, many media observers were concerned about the television coverage of the Gulf War. Every evening we sat at home and watched SMART bombs pass the windows of the reporters' hotels. The war became a fascinating display of western military equipment. The shocking statistics of death were lost in the science of war.

One study on television violence found that the more screen violence a subject saw the more they had an exaggerated sense of danger and mistrust. They also had difficulty distinguishing between fact and fantasy. This is particularly relevant since many abusers resort to violence after falsely accusing their partner of unfaithfulness and other unacceptable behaviour. The abuser may see himself as being threatened when in fact there is no reason for him to feel that way. A victim may not understand how he can possibly suspect her of such things.

This study would indicate that this may be, at least partly, attributable to violent forms of entertainment.

Is it relevant that men are more powerful than women in general?

Many feminists who have researched domestic violence believe that it does stem from the fact that men are more powerful than women in society in general. Obviously, most men are physically more powerful than women. However, they also dominate in politics and are more likely to hold positions at the top of major companies than are women. On average, men still earn more then women. Even some churches refuse women access to any positions of leadership and authority, leaving these solely for the men. Women are characterized as childcarers and homemakers. The word 'patriarchal' describes societies such as ours which are based on male leadership and dominance.

In some families this can be taken to extremes. As Jenny said:

He thought he was man of the house and that meant I was his slave. He made decisions and I was to do what he said. If his tea wasn't just right, or if there was dust on a shelf, I'd get a belt to 'teach me a lesson'.

It could be that some abusers use violence—whether consciously or not—to reinforce their belief that men are the boss and should be in control. The fact that the woman is often in the weaker position makes it all the easier for the abuser to take this position. If the cost of childcare makes it not worth a woman's while to take the low-paid jobs which would be available to her, then he may be the sole breadwinner. This makes it easier for him to claim, for example, that household money will be spent as he sees fit, and harder for the wife to do anything about it if she is not given enough money to care for the children adequately. It also makes it harder for her to leave an abusive relationship.

Does it have anything to do with the status of the abuser?

Another theory says that families are prone to domestic violence when the abuser's status or position is perceived by him as being lower than it should be. There could be a number of reasons for this:

His partner has a higher education than he does and is seen by others as 'the smart one'. He may feel that this makes him inferior to her, whereas he should be the leader of the relationship.

He is made unemployed and his partner is now the main breadwinner. He may believe that he should be the one to take care of the family.

The abuser is highly qualified—perhaps an accountant or a teacher—but at present he can get only a menial job.

There was a chance for him to be promoted at work but the position was given to a much younger man, from whom he now has to take orders.

The theory suggests that when an abuser finds himself in a situation like this it creates within him conflicts and stresses which he is unable to cope with in any other way than to be violent. If this seems to be the situation in a particular family, it is important for the victim to realize that the fact that an abuser finds himself in such a situation does not excuse his violence. Disappointments in life do not provide a justification for ruining someone else's life.

The situation does not actually cause the violence. It is not because the victim earns more than her partner that he abuses her. It is because he has misplaced ideas about the male role in a relationship—he may not understand that marriage or cohabitation is a mutual sharing of domestic responsibilities, as circumstances allow.

Resorting to violence because circumstances and the abuser's own beliefs cause frustration in him is not acceptable. There are other ways to resolve tension and it is up to an abuser to learn other ways of coping with stress. Again, it is not a victim's fault that he responds with violence.

Surely it depends on the character of the man himself?

It is true that the personality and individual character of an abuser may shed some light on his behaviour. Abusers have an individual responsibility for their violence, no matter what influences have been placed on them. So, looking at an abuser as an individual rather than just as a member of a group of men who abuse is important. Research shows that many abusers:

have low self-esteem
feel powerless and inadequate
believe in stereotyping of men and women
tend to blame others for their actions
are jealous
have poor responses to stressful situations
do not believe their violent behaviour should have
   negative consequences for them.

Alone, these characteristics do not explain why a man is an abuser. A man may have some or all of them and still not participate in domestic violence. However, if these characteristics are combined with other factors then they may give us an understanding of why a particular man is violent. For example, Shelly said of her husband Bobby:

Bobby was brought up in a very strict family. His father's word was law. A man was there to provide for the wee woman at home. Bobby lost his job and I took in childminding to meet the bills. Because I worked from home, caring for small children, I started to set out house rules to ensure everything worked out and the children were safe. With hindsight, the violence started around that time. He felt everything was the wrong way round and he resented my strong position.

Bobby was in a situation where the roles had been reversed and his wife was now the person who contributed most to the finances and had the most say about how the house was run. Bobby could have reacted differently. He could have appreciated his wife's support at a difficult time and supported her in her own new role, which she found tiring and demanding. However, his own character and the values which were instilled into him by his parents made that difficult. He didn't see the new situation as just an inevitable side effect of the recession. He felt powerless and inadequate—as if it was his fault he was not being the breadwinner. He didn't believe that it was right that his wife should finance the family or tell him how the house was run, and perhaps he even felt jealous of her being able to work. His poor response to the stress his feelings caused meant that instead of going for a run or talking to a friend to get rid of the tension, he would hit Shelly. Shelly felt that he thought that was an acceptable way of 'bringing her down to size' and that he wasn't doing anything wrong.

Does family background have any influence?

It does seem that violent behaviour can be passed down through the generations. A study of 4,000 abused women in New York City found that 80% of the abusers were either abused themselves as children or observed abuse against their own mothers.

Children will model their behaviour on their parental role models. If their experience of family life is that daddy hitting mummy is as common as having cornflakes for breakfast then it is likely that they will grow up to repeat this violent behaviour in their own adult relationships. A male will be more likely to hit his female partners. It is also possible that a female child who witnesses violence at home may be less likely to reject as a partner someone whom she knows or suspects will be violent towards her. Until someone tells the adults that this violence is not acceptable, they may not have any other expectation. Violence will be seen as normal family life. However, not every boy who sees his mother abused will himself become an abuser. Some men are so distressed by their father's behaviour that they vow never to be like him. Again, it all depends on the individual.

Do they do it simply because it suits them?

Violent behaviour may be reinforced when an abuser realizes that the violence achieves what he wants—in the short term at least. If it works, he will do it again. Jody said:

He hated me going round to see Mary, even though we'd been at school together. Eventually, every time I got home he would hit me. It just wasn't worth it and in the end I stopped seeing her.

Maria found that her whole outlook on life changed.

I was a really loud, outgoing person when I met him. He was quiet and retiring but I liked that in him at first—I thought he was the dependable type. But as we went on it became clear to me that he was getting annoyed with me being the way I was. I think he felt that I was getting all the attention and he couldn't compete with me. As time went on he started to be violent to me and he made it clear he wanted me to calm down and be the quiet little woman at home. At first I resisted and carried on going out to parties and clubs. The violence got worse and worse—it started out with a few pushes and shoves. Within a few years I had been in hospital four times with broken bones. He got what he wanted though. I stopped going out with friends—I was too scared of what he'd do when I got in. At home he was like a bear with a sore head, so I wouldn't say anything in case it made him flare up again. I even cut myself off from my family. When I did eventually leave him everyone told me how much I had changed. It took months before I felt right even going to a pub.

The other point to be made here is that 'People hit and abuse family members because they can.' [1] An abuser may be fairly sure that his victim will not take any action against him, be that for love, fear, or ignorance of her options. For many reasons, the victim may feel powerless to ensure that her abuser's violence has negative consequences for him. Thus, the benefits of the violence are more than the costs and he is likely to carry on.

Is there a spiritual reason for the violence?

Some victims of domestic violence may not believe in God. Others, however, may have religious beliefs which cause them to ask whether their religion has any answers for them. Religious leaders may say that domestic violence is just one example of how a society which has turned its back on God has begun to disintegrate. Christianity's teaching includes the following messages to the victim of domestic violence:

Each person is worthy in God's sight. He sent his Son to die for the whole of humanity because he loves each person equally. So, no matter what an abuser may say

of you, in Christianity's teaching it is not possible for
you to be worthless or useless.

Marriage is a good thing. It is not God's plan that the
female should be completely dominated by the man.
One old ditty says that Eve was created out of the rib
of Adam so that she was, 'not from the head of Adam
that she might rule him, not from the feet of Adam
that she may be walked on by him, but from his side,
close to his heart that she should be loved by him'.

God hates it when marriages are split up and when
violence mars them. In Malachi 2:16 he says
specifically:

'I hate divorce... and I hate a man's covering his
wife with violence as with his garment.'

In biblical times a man's covering his wife with a
garment was symbolic of the protection and care
which he would give her as a husband. So this
verse means that God hates it when that caring
relationship is spoilt by violence against the wife.

So, it may be of some comfort to victims who believe in God
to know that he does not condone the violence. It is not
something which he expects you to endure. It could be said
that the whole root of domestic violence is that the abusers are
not living according to the principles set out in the Bible, which
promotes non-violent relationships. Of course, the Bible also
gives a message of hope—that with the help of God an abuser
who wishes to change his behaviour can repent and become a
new man.

Clearly, it is not easy to say precisely why each abuser is
violent. Domestic violence is a complex issue which involves
both the way our whole society operates and the individual
character and beliefs of the abuser. However, considering all
these ideas gives victims some important things to hold on
to:

It is not your fault you are being abused.

Your abuser may do it because of the way he was brought up or because of the way that others have taught him how to behave. However, he is still responsible for the way he behaves. He cannot blame it all on someone else.

The reasons your abuser is violent may be very complicated. He may not fully understand them himself. However, because there are reasons—however obscure—it means that he can get help if he wants to change. A later chapter deals with how he can do this.

God has not abandoned you to a life of violence with no hope. He does not condone the violence and will not condemn you for seeking to stop it or for seeking to get protection for you and your children.

1. Gelles and Cornell, Intimate Violence in Families,1985, p. 120.

CHAPTER 4

Am I wrong to stay?

Why don't women in violent relationships simply leave the home? Why do they stay and put up with the abuse day after day, month after month?

These are questions which many people who are just learning about domestic violence ask. The assumption behind the question may be that the violence cannot be all that bad, or the victim would not tolerate it. Or else they may believe that the victim actually enjoys the violence and that is why she stays. In fact there are many reasons why a victim may still be living with her abuser. Often any number of these reasons combine to keep the victim in the relationship.

The side effects of the violence itself

As this chapter will show, leaving a violent relationship is not just a question of walking out of the front door into a perfect new life. A victim who wants to leave will have many practical and emotional matters to deal with—housing, finance, loneliness, fear, childcare, schooling and so on. Any person who has ever had to move house will know how many practical matters need to be sorted out and what a stressful time it can be. On top of all that the victim will have to deal with all the emotions which accompany being abused and also the break-up of an intimate relationship. She will have to cope with all this at a time when she is at her most vulnerable because of the violence.

One of the long-term effects of being constantly abused is the psychological paralysis a victim may experience. The Women's Aid Federation (England) Research Group said:

> The constant pressures of the violent situation are debilitating. The experience of pain, confusion and humiliation leads to a paralysis which is not easily shed. Beyond the initial confusion, apathy and despair, we noticed a continuing loss of confidence, energies and initiative, an inability to cope with officialdom and difficulty in making decisions.[1]

In other words, the very fact that they have suffered domestic violence can make leaving difficult. It is a little bit like a man who is trapped in a burning building. He is shouting out of the window to passers-by that the heat is hurting him. 'Well, why doesn't he just get out of the building?' they ask. Of course, it is the heat of the fire which prevents him escaping. It can be the same for a victim of domestic violence. One of my clients expressed it well when she said:

> My head was just cabbaged with him. I'd start to do something and then I'd find I'd just stood there for half an hour, watching out of the window to see if he was coming back. I couldn't concentrate on nothing—it was like having scrambled egg in my head!

There is a theory known as the 'theory of learned helplessness' which has a similar message. This says that if a person is in a home where the only messages she hears about herself come from one person, then she is likely to accept what that person says. So, if an abuser keeps a woman isolated and constantly tells her that she is useless and stupid, then she is likely to come to think about herself that way. This is especially so when the message is reinforced with violence as 'punishment' for her stupidity. A woman who believes she is stupid and useless is unlikely to believe that she has the ability to cope on her own if she left her abuser.

Leaving a home takes an immense amount of self-confidence and courage. This must be found at the same time as the abuser is systematically destroying those qualities in the victim. It is not surprising many victims feel unable to leave.

The cycle of violence

Domestic violence tends to follow a cyclical pattern which itself makes it harder for a woman to leave the relationship. A violent incident is typically followed by a period of repentance. The abuser is sorry for his actions and promises to change. He seeks to convince her that it will all be different in the future and may beg for her forgiveness. If the woman accepts this and stays with him there then follows a honeymoon period when the relationship is at its best and all appears well. However, as time goes on the tension builds up again until there is another violent incident and the cycle begins to repeat itself. This cycle may happen slowly or take place more than once in a day.

The problem for the victim is that the most logical time for her to leave is just after the violent incident. At this time the abuse is strongest in her mind and the motivation for leaving is at its strongest. However, it is also at this time that the debilitating effects of that violence are at their strongest. By the time she recovers from the immediate shock of the abuse and gathers her thoughts towards the practical aspects of leaving the home, her abuser is likely to have moved into his repentance stage and the relationship will be moving towards the honeymoon period. This is the stage at which the woman has most cause for hope—which is, after all, what she is likely to be seeking when she is considering whether to leave or to stay. When the relationship is going well it is easier to believe that the previous incident was really the last one, that her abuser will keep his promise to change. So she stays—and the violence begins again, spinning her deeper into the trap of domestic violence. In other words, the cycle means that she has to leave at a time when, paradoxically, she has the least reason to.

Fear of retaliation

Many abusers deliberately discourage their victims from leaving by threatening them with what they will do if they try it:

> **'If you leave me I will find you and kill you.'**
> **'If you leave me you will never see your children again.'**
> **'If you leave me I will scar you so badly no other man will ever look at you again.'**

Some victims pluck up the courage to leave, only to find that their abuser finds them and carries out his threats, causing them to return to the home. To think about leaving again is doubly hard—they know only too well the consequences of attempting to do so. Victims may not know that they can get protection by a court order to keep them safe once they have left. They may not know how to go about getting safe accommodation where they cannot be traced. Even if they have this knowledge it can take some time to pluck up the courage to overcome the fear and to step out into the unknown.

A victim may feel that as long as she is in her own home she understands how the abuser will behave. She can predict when he will be violent and she may feel she can cope better with it in a familiar house. She may feel that if she leaves, the situation will become unpredictable and thus more frightening. One counsellor I spoke to said that she had met women who knew how to live only with violence. Peace was unknown to them, and when they left they found themselves unable to cope with it.

Love of her partner

The woman would not be in the relationship in the first place if she had not at some time felt strongly for her partner. It is not uncommon for a woman to continue to love her partner despite the violence. He may be a good partner in other ways. Perhaps he is particularly fond of the children and kind to the wife except when he is drinking, or except at the weekend. Perhaps he has not always been violent—in many relationships the violence only manifests itself after marriage or after a pregnancy. So often when women come to see me they ask, 'Do I have to go through with the divorce once I get an injunction out against him? What if it works and he just sees sense and stops hitting me? That's all I want really.'

In fact they do not have to get a divorce to be protected by a court order. It is not unrealistic for a woman to want this to be just a bad patch which they are going through and for the violence to stop but the relationship to continue. She may hope that the shock of her having taken court proceedings—or even just initial legal advice—will be enough to shock him into stopping the violence. Again, many women say to me, 'I just don't think he realizes how bad things have got. Perhaps he will realize I'm serious if I do this. I've got to do something to make him see what he is doing to me.'

A woman may feel that it is only her continued support which will give her partner the strength to change. She may feel that she has to be there to support him though counselling or his period of stress. She may hold to a traditional view of marriage—that she should stand by her man. If a woman feels this way, then to suggest that she is wrong to stay is to ask her to abandon all hope for the relationship. In fact this may not be an appropriate thing to do. Later chapters show how couples can get help to save their relationships from violence.

Religious or family pressure

Other women feel that they have lost all love for their abuser. They may feel that the relationship is at an end and that it will never be revived. Or they may feel they still love their abuser but their own physical safety demands that they leave. Yet they may also feel pressurized by church or family into staying.

The Christian marriage ceremony contains the words, 'For better or for worse'. Religious circles or parents with very traditional views may take this to mean that the woman should stay in her marriage despite the violence. Otherwise she is breaking her solemn vows. Indeed, the woman herself may hold these views in principle and find herself in a no-win situation. It may be her strong religious faith which is sustaining her through the suffering as it is. The thought that she could lose the approval of her God and her church associates may be too much for her to bear. That could be a worse scenario for her than the continued violence.

Concern for her children

A woman may choose to stay in a violent relationship for the sake of the children. Perhaps the violence is not directed at the children and the abuser is otherwise a good father to them. A later chapter will deal with the effects of parental violence on children in the same home, and discuss the evidence that children are in fact damaged by just watching violence. However, a mother may feel that she cannot deny her children the benefits of living with both their parents. Indeed, her children may put pressure on her not to leave their dad if they do not fully appreciate the situation. As another client said to me, 'If I leave, the children leave too. They lose their school, their friends, their bedroom and their playmates. Why should they suffer for the way he is? No, let him leave.' She instructed me to seek a court order forcing him to leave the home and protecting her from further abuse from him.

Alternatively, a victim may genuinely fear losing her children if she leaves the home. She may fear that the social services will think her a bad mother for taking them to a refuge and will take them into care. Or her abuser may tell her that if she leaves he will fight her through the courts for the children. In extreme cases he may even threaten to kill the children and himself if she leaves. There have been enough newspaper reports of fathers who have done this to make it a real fear in some mothers' minds. A woman may simply not feel able to risk losing her children. (See Chapter 7 for a further discussion of these fears.)

Self-blame

We have already seen that victims often blame themselves for the violence. A woman who is still thinking in this way may not feel it appropriate to leave the relationship. She may feel that she ought to stay and change her behaviour so that she doesn't cause the violence any more.

Also, in our society women are frequently viewed in the light of their relationships with men. A woman who has a contented marriage and good children is seen as a success. On the other hand, if a relationship breaks down some people will always blame the woman, no matter what the background to the situation. A successful career woman—perhaps bringing up children on her own—is often still not seen as an ideal woman because she has not been able to sustain a relationship with a man. A woman may believe this herself and thus think that if she leaves she will be a failure. Reluctant to fail, she will decide to stay and work it out.

Alternatively, a woman who does not share those beliefs may still be afraid that others who do will look down on her. This

61

might be especially difficult if her family and close friends are likely to look at the situation in that way. If a woman is seeking to escape a situation where she is made to feel inferior and a failure, she may consider that leaving would put her in the same position and is thus not a solution.

Financial dependence

So often women are financially dependent on their abuser. We have seen how this may be a deliberate ploy on the part of the abuser. Or it may be that the woman is unable to work because she has small children or because she has no qualifications. Or perhaps she lives in a rural area, or an area of high unemployment, where her chances of getting work are slim. She may not be aware of her entitlement to welfare benefits if she leaves, or she may know how low an income she would be on if she left the home, and decide that this would make her children suffer unacceptably.

She may also know that if she leaves it will have to be overnight, without warning, to avoid retaliation. She will be unable, in those circumstances, to take any furniture or household items with her. If she is rehoused by the council elsewhere, how will she furnish the house on income support? She may not know of her rights in law or may feel unable to pursue a financial action through the courts. Thus, she may feel that she cannot afford to leave the home.

Immigration law and community loss

Women who belong to ethnic minorities may have additional pressures placed on them. If they have entered this country within the last year, only to find themselves married to a violent man, immigration laws may prevent them leaving him without putting their presence in this country at risk. This problem was highlighted by a delegate from Southhall Black Sisters at a Victim Support conference on domestic violence. She explained:

> *The one year rule requires that immigration applicants remain in marriage for one year before being given indefinite leave to stay in Britain... The one year rule makes women entirely dependent on their spouses, economically, socially, physically and emotionally. They risk being deported if they leave violent relationships before their immigration status is made secure. They cannot claim public assistance (benefits, housing and so on) before their status is settled. Southhall Black Sisters know of cases where, because of these requirements, women are forced to endure violence and abuse.[2]*

Women may also come from communities where there is great shame on women who leave marriages or who live outside of the extended family. The community may in fact support the abuser and place great pressure on the victim to stay 'for the honour of her family'. To leave the relationship then requires the victim to leave her community as well, which forces the victim into a situation of isolation and loneliness. Religion may play a part in this if the victim's religion places a great emphasis on marriage or the extended family. Recent immigrants may also have language or literacy problems which make it harder for them to deal with the practical problems of leaving a home and living alone.

Homelessness

Many a woman in a violent relationship feels that she has nowhere else to go. Perhaps there are no relatives or friends to whom she can turn for a bed. Perhaps she feels the need to move right out of the area if she is to leave, but all her family accommodation. Or perhaps the local refuge is full at present and the nearest place is so far away she would not be able to get back for her work. Or again, perhaps she has a refuge place offered to her but is not yet ready to take the plunge of moving into this type of accommodation. Perhaps she is afraid of what it will be like there, never having experienced this form of communal living. If she has children she will have their needs to consider.

On the other hand, she might have somewhere to go in the short term but be worried about where she is to live in the long term. Perhaps she has invested all her money into the house and is reluctant to let her abuser take all the benefit of it. Chapter 5 deals with court action to preserve a victim's existing property, but not many victims are aware of the provisions without legal advice. Even then court action can be protracted and stressful, and success cannot be guaranteed at the outset.

The fact that a woman thinks like this does not mean that she is materialistic or that the violence is not severe enough to frighten her. It is more that leaving home with nowhere to go—especially if children are involved—is a big step. Finding out about new accommodation is not easy and can require a lot of time and energy, which many victims do not have.

Information gathering

A woman may still be in the violent relationship for the time being, but be in the process of finding out how she can leave. There are so many things to consider that this may take her some time. Groups offering help to victims frequently find that women will take their information but will act on it only weeks, months or even years later. It may be that it takes the woman a long time to lay down the practical plans for leaving. She may delay for practical reasons—perhaps in a year's time her eldest child is due to change schools anyway and she has decided to wait until then to keep the disruption to a minimum. Or perhaps she knows her husband is due to go away on a training course in three months' time, which will give her the chance to leave and get a head start on him before he realizes. Or the victim may simply be gathering her courage and making sure in her own mind that she is making the right decision to abandon her relationship.

The right to choose

It should not be assumed that women who have stayed in a violent relationship beyond the first and second assaults will never leave. Women often seek help after years of abuse. Often, to an outsider, nothing distinguishes the violent episode which makes them leave from all the previous ones. Yet the woman has reached her own breaking-point. One punch may be the straw that breaks the camel's back.

Women who choose to stay should never be judged. It is exactly that—*their choice*. Help groups, such as Women's Aid, place great emphasis on the woman retaining her choice. So much of domestic violence is about taking away the victim's dignity and right to make decisions. Part of the restoration of victims' lives is to recognize their right to choose. This includes the right to choose to endure violence for any of the reasons mentioned above.

Support is still available for women who choose to stay in the home. It need not be a choice between staying and help. You can have both. The rest of this book will give you some idea of what is available to you if you are in this position. For now, if you are still in a relationship and are thinking about leaving, it may help you to consider the following points:

**Think about why you are staying. Read through this
book and, when you know more about the choices
which are open to you, think again about why you are**

which are open to you, think again about why you are really staying. If it is because you really want to, then you have a perfect right to do so. If it is because you thought it was impossible for you to leave, look into some of the sources of help available to you. Later, when you have had a chance to see how things could be, think about it again. The choice is still yours, but the situation may not be as bleak as you think.

You can stay and get help. You may not feel it right to leave the home. Still, do not suffer in silence. Talk to someone about your problem and see how you can get support while you are in the home.

As Chapter 2 showed you, you are not on your own in this situation. If you don't know where to start to get help, contact one or more of the organizations listed in Appendix 1. They will be able to put you in touch with someone locally who will help you.

If you feel that you are under religious pressure to stay in your marriage, remember that most religious leaders, while supporting marriage, would not condemn you to a life of misery because of physical abuse. Talk to your church leader about it. It is possible for the violence to be dealt with and for you to get support without necessarily getting divorced. Indeed, dealing with the violence instead of ignoring it is a positive way to support marriage. If the violence is ignored the marriage is a weak one anyway—the parties do not have the true intimacy and mutual support for which marriage was intended. If your leader believes that your abuser is right then consider speaking to another religious leader. It will be possible for you to find help elsewhere without having to leave the church altogether—many clergy are now sympathetic to the victims of domestic violence. Remember—marriage is in God's plans, but violence in marriage is not.

Whether you decide to stay or to leave, use the safety plan at the back of this book (Appendix 3) to help maximize your safety and to help you cope with any further violence.

1. The Women's Aid Federation (England) Research Group, 1981, p. 13.
2. Pragna Patel, 'Domestic Violence—Breaking the Cycle', report of a Victim Support one-day conference, 21 April 1993.

CHAPTER 5

Is the law on my side?

The phrase 'a rule of thumb' originates from the old English law that a husband could beat his wife as long as the stick he used was no wider than his own thumb. Thankfully, the laws in England and Wales have changed considerably since then.[1] In the 1970s specific laws were introduced, allowing victims of domestic violence to get court orders protecting them from their abusers. While this book was being written, the Family Law Act 1996 was passed. The Act introduces improvements to the protection that the civil legal system gives to victims. It will be some time before this law comes into force, however. This chapter has therefore been written in general terms so that it will remain applicable.

England and Wales

Victims can apply for a court order against their abusers. The content of that order will necessarily depend on the circumstances of the case and the law in force at the time of the application. However, there are three main areas which a court order can cover. In all these cases, an order can include the children's names as the people who are protected, where violence or harassment has previously been directed at them. Orders also routinely forbid the abuser from getting anyone else to do the forbidden acts on his behalf.

(a) Molestation

Molestation is a legal term which covers any form of harassment or pestering of the victim, such as:

verbal abuse

unwanted letters or telephone calls

continually turning up at the victim's property

deliberately spreading lies about the victim

smashing furniture

anything else which is calculated to intimidate or upset the victim.

The court will want to know that there has been some previous molestation before making a court order.

(b) Violence

An order can also forbid the abuser from using or threatening to use violence against the victim. Again, the court will want some evidence of previous violence to justify an order. However, where there has not been actual violence in the past but threats have been made, the courts are usually agreeable to forbidding the use of violence in the future.

(c) Home occupation

In serious cases the court can order that an abuser leaves the home he shares with the victim, or an order can be made requiring the abuser to allow the victim to return to a property he has caused her to leave. The courts can also order, in certain cases, that an abuser does not approach the place where the victim is now living.

How do I get a court order?

It is possible to act in person and take proceedings without legal advice. If you are doing this you can take what is known as a 'McKenzie friend' [2] into court with you. A McKenzie friend is any non-lawyer who is going to help you run your court case. They cannot conduct the case for you but can sit next to you and advise you on what to say.

However, most victims will want to be represented in court by a solicitor. It is possible simply to choose a solicitor at random and most firms will have at least one member of staff who will do this kind of work. However, to be sure that you get a solicitor who will represent you well, you may want to make some enquiries about the people who work locally to you. Citizens' Advice Bureaux, police domestic violence units, women's groups and other local agencies will all be able to recommend a selection of suitable solicitors. Alternatively, ask people you know to be in the same situation for personal recommendations. Firms who hold a Legal Aid Franchise have also passed quality tests and so should offer a good service.

How will I pay for it?

Getting a court order can happen very quickly because the courts will treat domestic violence cases as urgent. Nevertheless, the costs can easily run into several hundred pounds because the work a solicitor does can be time-intensive. So how can a victim fund a court case?

Free first interviews
Many firms of solicitors will give you a free interview at the beginning for fifteen or thirty minutes. This allows you to find out how the law applies to your case, whether you qualify for

legal aid and, if not, how much it will cost you to go ahead. Ask when making an appointment with a solicitor if they will do this for you. Shop around until you find one who will.

'Green Form' legal aid

If you are on certain welfare benefits, such as income support, or have a very low income, then you will qualify for Green Form advice and assistance. This is a legal aid form which a solicitor can get you to sign at your first interview. It will give them a limited amount of time to advise you. If you qualify you will not have to pay for any work done under this form. A Green Form covers initial advice and correspondence but will not cover court proceedings.

Full legal aid certificate

To take proceedings to court on legal aid a solicitor will have to apply for a full legal aid certificate for you. This is means-tested and you can qualify for this form of legal aid with a much higher income than for Green Form advice. Depending on your income you may have to make a monthly contribution to the certificate. If an order for costs is made against your opponent and those costs are actually paid then you may get your contributions back, but this is never guaranteed.

A legal aid application for domestic violence cases will be made on an emergency basis. A solicitor should always explain to you in detail how the legal aid scheme works. It is quite complicated, so it is entirely acceptable to ask questions about it if you are not sure how it applies to you.

Paying privately

If you do not qualify for legal aid then you will have to pay a solicitor privately. If this is the case, make sure you get the following from them at the initial interview:

a rough estimate of your total costs

**an explanation of how they will charge you. Solicitors
work on an hourly charging rate, on top of which you
will have to pay for VAT and any disbursements the
solicitor pays for on your behalf, such as court fees
and the fees of a bailiff to serve court papers**

**confirmation of when you will have to pay the money
and whether you can pay in instalments.**

What happens if I decide to go ahead?

How quickly you can obtain an order depends on the
seriousness of the situation. The two following stories are
typical of what might happen if you wish to obtain a court
order.

Although no one should have to tolerate any level of
domestic violence, Maggie's case was one of the less serious I
had come across. She had had a relationship with a man named
Gary for two years although they had never lived together.
Throughout that time her boyfriend had shown that he had a
violent temper. He had hit her on one or two occasions and had
smashed up some of the furniture in her lounge during an
argument. As a result she ended the relationship and made it
clear to him that she did not want him to visit her at her home
any more. The only exception was that they had a one-year-old
daughter, and she arranged for Gary to collect the child at the
same time every weekend so that he could spend the weekend
with her.

At first this arrangement worked well. Maggie thought that
she had begun to put her past behind her and that the
relationship—although a mistake—was over. However, after
three weeks or so, Gary began to pester her. He would ring up
to speak to her about the child, despite the fact that

arrangements had already been made. He would use that as an excuse to try and persuade her to come back to him. When she refused and repeated that the relationship was over he would become abusive to her, calling her unpleasant names and accusing her of being a bad mother. On several of these occasions he threatened to use violence on her.

About six weeks after they split up, Maggie accepted an invitation from an old school friend, whom she had met by chance, to go out for a drink. She returned home at midnight and sent the babysitter home. At three o'clock in the morning she received an enraged phone call from Gary. He said that if he ever saw her going out with another man again he would put a hammer through her head and would have her daughter taken into care. She realized at that point that he must have been watching her house. She told him again that the relationship was over.

Two days later, he arrived at her property and banged on the front door, yelling and shouting that he was going to kill her and that he would have his own way in the end. Maggie refused to answer the door to him but shouted down from the window that he should go away. He refused to do so, so she called the police but by the time they arrived he had gone.

Two days later, having thought about it, she came to see me to see if the law could protect her in any way. She was claiming income support and so she would qualify for legal aid. However, I had to consider whether the Legal Aid Board would consider the merits of her case strong enough. As the law stood, I had to advise her that the Board was likely to refuse her legal aid unless we wrote a warning letter to Gary first. This was because he had not actually used violence on her, except a long time ago. We therefore wrote him a stiff letter, telling him that if he did not stop bothering her then we would apply for a court order.

Three days later, Maggie returned to my office. The day he had received the letter, Gary had telephoned her four times, shouting abuse down the phone and threatening to kill her.

Since we had tried a letter first, I advised her we should now apply for legal aid. We filled the forms in and they were sent in the courier system to the Legal Aid Board that night. Late the next day we received a fax from the Board, saying that the application had been granted.

The next step was therefore to draft all the court papers. These included a statement which gave an account of all that had happened in the past—everything which Maggie had told me. I telephoned Maggie and she came in that afternoon. She checked that all the details on the paperwork were correct and then we went to the local court office to issue the application. She swore an oath on the Bible to say that the statement was true. A statement sworn in this way is known as an affidavit.

The court officials gave us a date for the hearing in three days' time. This was because a certain amount of time was needed to give Gary notice of the hearing. We took the papers back to the office and arranged for a private detective to serve the application on Gary. This was done so that the courts were sure that he had notice of the hearing—if the private detective swears an affidavit to say that he handed the papers to Gary, there can be no doubt.

The hearing soon came. Maggie met me at my office and we walked over together, so she would never be on her own with him. We waited for him until ten minutes past the appointment time, but he didn't turn up. So we went before a district judge, gave him the private detective's affidavit, and told him that all the evidence was in Maggie's own affidavit. This meant that she did not have to give any evidence in court. The district judge made an order that Gary should not harass her, pester her or otherwise molest her, that he should not threaten or use violence on her, and that he should not try to enter or actually enter her property. This order was made to last for three months.

Again, after the hearing the order was served on Gary by the private detective. An order is only effective from the time it is served and so we asked the private detective to find him as soon as possible. In this case he went to a local pub, where we knew Gary drank, and served the order on him there. The private detective told us Gary was so displeased that he threw his pint over him—but at least we knew that Maggie was now protected.

Since Gary was told about the first hearing in advance, this procedure was known as an 'on notice application'. In some cases, giving the man notice that his victim was taking him to court would put the woman in more danger of violence, and so an emergency procedure can be used. Sheila's case was a prime example of this.

Sheila had married when she was only eighteen and had put up with violence throughout most of her seven-year marriage. Steve, her husband, had kicked, punched, bitten and thumped her on a regular basis—even while she was pregnant. In the week before she came to see me she had had a knife held to her throat, had an iron thrown at her head and been beaten on three occasions—once in front of friends because she had not had any decaffeinated coffee in the house, only normal Nescafé. She couldn't say what had made her seek help at this stage rather than earlier. She just said that she had had enough.

As I talked to her it became apparent that as well as the physical violence he controlled her with threats. One of his constant threats was that if she told anyone he would kill her. Because of this threat, and because of the seriousness of the violence, it was obvious that we should use the emergency procedure known as an '*ex parte* application'—*ex parte* being Latin for 'without the other party'. By this time, I was working for a firm with a Legal Aid Franchise. This meant that a partner in the firm was able to grant her legal aid in-house on the same day.

The papers were prepared in the same way as for Maggie and we went over to the court. However, this time, instead of being given a date in the future we were given the court file and told to go straight up and see a district judge there and then, even though we did not have an appointment. As a result we had to wait until he was free, but were soon called in to see him.

This time the district judge did want to hear a little bit from Sheila. He asked her one or two questions just to clarify her affidavit, then granted an order which was to last for two weeks. We had asked for an order removing Steve from the house, but he refused to grant this until Steve had notice of the application. He did grant Sheila an injunction in the same terms as Maggie's order though, to protect her while she was in the house. We took the file down to the office again and they listed the matter for another hearing in a week's time. The order was then served on Steve.

At the return hearing Steve turned up. He had been to see a solicitor but he did not get legal aid and so decided to come and contest the order himself. There was therefore a longer hearing. Sheila had to give a little bit of evidence—just to expand on her statement, and so that the judge could see how frightened and genuinely scared she was. The judge then gave Steve a chance to tell his side of the story. His statements were clearly unbelievable and contradictory. I cross-examined him a little bit, but the district judge was soon convinced that the order should be granted. He made an order in the same terms as before and added that Steve should leave the house in the next three days. Since he was at court and knew about the order, the judge also gave us permission to serve a copy of the order by post this time.

Undertakings

In Maggie and Sheila's cases the partner either didn't bother to come to court or came and defended the application. However, there is a middle way which many abusers take. This is to give an undertaking to the court.

An abuser rarely gets legal aid to defend an application. This is because the Legal Aid Board says that most cases can be dealt with by undertakings and so the abuser will not be at any disadvantage if he does not have a lawyer with him at the court. An undertaking is a promise to the court not to do the things he is accused of. It means that he does not admit his past behaviour, and the court does not go through all the evidence. It means a quicker hearing and in some cases offers as good protection to the victim as a court order. In some cases it is not as good, and a solicitor should advise you about whether to accept any undertaking which is being offered.

What if he breaks a court order or an undertaking?

The method of enforcing court orders and undertakings will change with the new law. However, in essence there are two methods. On some orders a power of arrest can be attached. (This is likely to be even more common under the new law.) If this is done then the police can arrest the abuser for a breach of the order and the matter will be brought back to court quickly. If a power of arrest is not attached then the victim can tell her solicitor about the breach of the order. Legal aid can be amended and the victim then applies to the court for an order that the abuser be committed to prison for contempt of court. Again, a solicitor should advise you fully on this.

Can the police help?

Traditionally, the police were seen as reluctant to intervene in situations of domestic violence. They would typically regard them as 'just family problems' and were reluctant to give victims much assistance. This was despite the fact that many episodes of domestic violence constitute criminal offences. Even those which are not crimes in themselves—such as general verbal harassment—can sometimes be classified as breaches of the peace, allowing the police to intervene. Where criminal charges are made police can often impose bail conditions, which give the victim protection without her having to take her own court proceedings.

The attitude of the police is now changing rapidly. In 1989 there was a Home Office circular which required police forces to set up specialist domestic violence units. These are now in operation and, while their methods of working vary slightly from location to location, they are now offering a good service to victims. These units have several purposes:

to provide a readily accessible and caring service within the police for individuals who have experienced domestic violence

to work with the police themselves to ensure a consistent approach

to train police officers and spread knowledge

to provide a contact point within the police so that other agencies can work together with them to improve services generally.

They try to follow up all incidents reported to the police, although they are often understaffed, and cannot deal with the problem as well as the officers working there would like. So, a victim who has called the police for assistance may find that an officer from the unit will approach her. Alternatively, a victim can go directly to her local domestic violence unit for help.

The units are able to advise a victim on whether to press criminal charges against an abuser and will support her through a court case if she chooses to do that. They can also provide advice on other sources of help. In some cases, the Legal Aid Board likes to know that the victim has approached the police for help before it will grant legal aid. The units also play a part in educating other officers in the area about domestic violence, with the result that the service of uniformed officers who respond to a 999 call has vastly improved. The police are the best port of call where a victim needs emergency help. If a victim obtains a court order it is useful if the solicitor sends a copy to the local police station, so that if there is an incident in the future, the officer investigating can radio in and get information on the background.

Scotland

Scotland runs a separate legal system to England and Wales. However, in relation to domestic violence the law is broadly similar. Some of the differences are:

The legal advice and assistance scheme in Scotland is a Pink Form rather than a Green Form.

Scottish law allows longer court orders than in England and Wales. For example, if a power of arrest is attached to a court order it will last until divorce, or until the order is withdrawn by the court. In England the general length of such a court order is three months.

The conditions in which a power of arrest can be attached to a court order differ from the old law in England, although if the new law does come into force the differences will be fewer.

Because the above information on English law avoids legal technicalities, it should give Scottish readers a good idea of what to expect from court hearings, apart from the above points of difference. In every case, in whichever country you live, it is important to seek legal advice to see just how the law applies to your particular case.

Financial applications

There are many ways in which the law can help an abused woman to come out of the relationship with an appropriate share of the family finances. Obviously, the law in this area is complex and this book cannot go into detail.

However, a married woman will be able to claim the following:

Maintenance from her husband for herself.

Child maintenance—this is now largely dealt with by the Child Support Agency rather than the courts, with some exceptions.

Capital—if there are any savings, insurance policies or pension funds, for example, a wife can claim her share of these.

House—if the matrimonial home is owned she can claim against this no matter whose name it is in. There are various orders which are possible in regard to the house:

Sometimes it is transferred to one partner outright.

In some cases one partner buys the other out, or it is sold and the proceeds divided.

In other cases, especially where there are children, the house is given to one partner for a set period—say until the youngest child is eighteen—and then it is sold and the proceeds divided.

If the couple agree, a court order can be made without a court hearing. However, if an abuser is determined to deny his victim her share in the matrimonial assets, the courts have all kinds of powers which a victim can use to make sure she receives what she should.

The situation is slightly different if the couple are not married. A women who lives with her abuser but is not married cannot claim maintenance from him for herself, but she can get child maintenance via the Child Support Agency. She can also claim her interest in the house if it is in joint names. Even if it is in her partner's sole name she may be able to claim an interest, for example if she has contributed to the deposit, or contributed indirectly to the property by doing rebuilding or refurbishing work. A woman in this position should always seek individual legal advice to see what her entitlements are. Other assets in joint names, such as policies or savings, can also be claimed against.

Conclusion

The law is not a magical power. In most cases, court orders make abusers think twice about what they are doing and the violence stops. Having said this, a court order cannot guarantee a cessation of abuse. However, a court can punish the abuser for a breach of an order in circumstances where nothing could have been done if there had been no order in place. The law is now on the side of the victim and can be a useful tool in giving the victim physical safety and peace of mind. The criminal law applies just as much to intimate partners as it does to strangers, and the police can assist victims more than ever. If you are considering legal action it may help you to remember the following:

The law can be expensive, but in many cases assistance is available. Seek free initial advice and insist on a full explanation of the cost implications.

The law can also be complicated. Never be afraid to ask questions and to make sure you know what is happening and why. It is easy for solicitors to use legal phrases and to forget that they are not commonly known. Do not feel stupid if you do not understand—ask.

Do not feel pressured into taking legal proceedings once you have sought advice. In many cases it will be the best thing for you to do, but it remains your choice. If you wish to delay proceedings or to stop a court case once you have started it, ask for advice on how that may affect your position in the future, then make up your own mind. Similarly, do not feel embarrassed to go for legal advice on more than one occasion. This is not at all uncommon.

1. The law in Scotland operates under a different system to that in England and Wales. This chapter deals with the main differences but all readers should seek individual legal advice on their own situations wherever they live.
2. Named after the case that established the principle.

CHAPTER 6

Who will hear my cry?

It is hard to deal with being in a violent relationship without help. Recognizing that you do not have to put up with violence is one thing. Doing something practical to change the situation is another entirely. We have seen that many women who want to leave feel that they cannot do so for practical reasons. Who will support them? Where will they live? What will they live off? To a victim trapped in an abusive relationship these worries can seem insurmountable.

In fact, help is available and there are people who will hear your cry. This chapter looks at some of the main sources of help available to victims of domestic violence.

Women's Aid

Women's Aid is one of the main organizations helping victims on a national basis. There are four national offices for England, Scotland, Northern Ireland and Wales, although they all offer broadly the same services. Welsh Women's Aid produces all its material in Welsh as well as English. The Women's Aid Federation England states its values and principles to be:

to believe women and children, and to prioritize their safety

to support women in taking control of their own lives

to recognize and care for the needs of children affected by violence

to promote equal opportunities and anti-discrimination in all its work and services.

The Women's Aid groups aim to work towards changing attitudes to domestic violence. They offer training and information and may run media campaigns. However, the majority of their day-to-day work involves caring for victims at a practical level. Shortages of funding and staffing mean that services available from Women's Aid groups around the country may vary. However, on the whole they aim to provide:

a safe place to stay
advice, information and support
help in obtaining permanent housing
counselling
activities and care for children and young people
outreach support for women who do not wish to leave their own homes or who have now moved out of a refuge but still need support
helplines
support with legal proceedings
welfare benefit advice.

A Women's Aid group is the ideal first port of call, as it will be able to advise you of all your options and of local agencies and services which will be available to you. It will also support you in seeking help from those sources, which can be invaluable as trailing from one office to another can undoubtedly be confusing and tiring if you have to do it alone.

Refuges

For a woman seeking to escape the violence, the first question is often 'Where can I go?' For those without family or friends who can put them up, the answer is often a refuge.

A refuge is primarily a safe place where a woman who is being abused can escape from the violence—either temporarily, or as a stepping-stone to leaving the relationship and building up a new life. Refuges can be run independently by individual charities—for example, the charity Refuge now runs what was the world's first domestic violence refuge in Chiswick, London. It also offers a national helpline. However, a large number of the refuges in the UK are run in connection with the Women's Aid movement.

Most refuges will accept any woman in need and her children, although there may be some restrictions relating to older male children. A refuge will not turn any woman away. If it is full, or if she wishes to move out of the area, a refuge can use a UK list to find a place elsewhere. Some refuges, however, offer a specialist service for women in certain minority groups. Amadudu in Liverpool, for example, offers specialist services to black women and women with black children. It also has bathroom facilities which are suitable for the special needs of Moslem women. Newham Asian's Women's Project has a name which speaks for itself. The Solas Anois refuge in London is aimed specifically at Irish women, including those from the travelling community, and aims to give a service which reflects these women's cultural backgrounds. Refuge has workers who speak Hindi, Punjabi and Gujarati and can provide interpreters. Other refuges are suitable for women with disabilities.

A refuge is a place where a woman can recover from the violence and start to make her own decisions about what she wishes to do in the future. Advice will be given where sought and support will be forthcoming. However, refuge workers will uphold a woman's right to make her own choices about how to deal with the violence. For that reason, women can stay for as long or as short a time as they need to and can return as often as they want.

The buildings themselves vary according to the funding available in a particular area. Usually each family will have its own rooms but common facilities such as the living rooms, play facilities, bathrooms and kitchen will be shared. Some refuges offer meals cooked by a chef, but in others women cook for themselves and their families. The important thing is that the refuges are secret locations and their addresses are not made available to the public. If a woman is tracked down to a particular refuge, she can be moved to another out of the area to ensure her safety.

Living a communal life at a time of stress can have its disadvantages. On the other hand, the support and friendship among the women there can strengthen a victim and equip her for her next move. Rachel spent several weeks in a refuge with her two young children before being rehoused.

At first I was just so relieved to be safe I could have been in a cowshed. I didn't realize I was so tired and I didn't really notice where I was for the first few days. Looking back, I think it was the kids who felt it the most. They whinged all the time, asking to go out, and it just wasn't safe. The workers and the other women helped me with them and tried to get them settled.

It was never a real home for us—we were all cramped into one room for a start, and living out of boxes. But it did do us good. The children made friends and my daughter still visits one girl she met there. After a bit they got used to it all. They opened out a lot and told me things about 'daddy being bad' I didn't realize they knew. For me, it was time to get my head together. I had counselling there—still do now—but just being able to talk to other adults who knew what I was on about was a tonic itself.

Don't get me wrong—after a while, we moved out of the refuge and got our own house. When that happened I was chuffed to bits. It seemed like a mansion after the refuge, and so quiet with just us. Living with strangers was not easy—there were one or two cat fights in the refuge. But I'm glad it was there for me when I needed it.

Local authority housing departments

In law, local authorities have a duty to rehouse anyone who is homeless because of domestic violence and is in 'priority need'. For this purpose you will be classed as homeless because of domestic violence if occupation of your existing accommodation will probably lead to violence from some other person living in it, or to threats of violence from someone who is living there and is likely to carry out the threats. Those who are deemed to have priority need are:

- **a pregnant woman or a person who lives with a pregnant woman**
- **a person with whom dependent children reside or might reasonably be expected to reside**
- **a person who is vulnerable as a result of old age, mental illness, handicap, physical disability or other special reason, or someone who lives with such a person or might reasonably be expected to live with such a person**
- **a person who is homeless or threatened with homelessness as a result of emergency such as fire, flood etc.**

It is a matter of the local authority's interpretation whether childless victims are in priority need. They can be classed as 'vulnerable' but this is at the authority's discretion.

If you are both homeless and in priority need then the local authority has a duty to find you temporary accommodation while they make further enquiries to enable them to give you permanent accommodation. Temporary shelter may be in a bed and breakfast on a short-term basis. Many councils will make use of local refuges to provide you with short-term accommodation. It is also possible to apply for housing out of your local area. The housing law says that the local authority in the area a victim flees to should take responsibility for her and should not send her back to her own area if the threat remains. However, it can practically be easier to be rehoused in a new area if the victim has some connection there, such as family.

The law also says that local authorities do not have to rehouse someone who makes herself homeless intentionally. This is defined as doing or not doing something which results in her ceasing to occupy accommodation which is available and in which she could reasonably have been expected to live. The guidance issued to local authorities does state that victims of domestic violence who leave the home to escape should not be treated as intentionally homeless. However, in practice, some local authorities may ask a victim to try and get an injunction before they will rehouse her. Local Women's Aid groups will be familiar with the requirements of your local authority.

Benefits

Chapter 5 deals with how a woman can take court action against her partner to ensure financial support. However, in cases where she does not wish to do so or where it is inappropriate for her to do so—for example, if he is unemployed and has no capital—there are welfare benefits which a victim with no income, or a very low income, can claim. These do not exactly allow for a luxurious lifestyle but do at least allow a victim to start again knowing she can provide the basics for herself and the children.

The rules and regulations on welfare benefits are complex and each claimant must be assessed individually to see what she is entitled to. However, the basic rules of eligibility for the most common benefits are as follows:[1]

Income support

To qualify you must:

be on a low income

not have savings and capital exceeding £8,000

not be in full-time work (full-time work is classed as 16 hours a week or more)

generally not be in full-time education

generally be at least 18

be available for work, unless you are in the categories of people who are excluded from this requirement (for example, carers of children).

Family credit

This is a tax-free benefit paid to low-waged earners with dependent children. To qualify you must:

be on a low income

not have savings and capital exceeding £8,000

live in Great Britain

work full-time (16 hours a week or more)

have at least one dependent child

not be on disability working allowance.

Housing benefit

This benefit to cover rent can be paid either alone or in conjunction with other benefits. To qualify you must:

be on a low income

not have savings exceeding £16,000

be liable to pay rent—this includes payments for hostels and bed and breakfast accommodation

normally occupy a property as your home

not be excluded by other rules.

There are certain regulations which would affect a victim of domestic violence. If you leave your normal home because of violence, this can affect your housing benefit entitlement in various ways:

If you go and live somewhere else on a temporary basis, where you are paying rent but you are intending to return to your normal home, the local authority can pay housing benefit for both properties for up to 52 weeks, if they think it is reasonable for them to do that. This might apply, for example, if you went to a refuge until you could get a court order getting your abuser out of the home.

If you go and stay somewhere else rent-free on a temporary basis and intend to return to your home, you can get housing benefit for your usual home for up to 52 weeks. This might apply if you went to stay with your mother just for a few weeks.

If you move out of your normal home permanently but cannot get out of paying the rent, then you can get housing benefit for your old house for up to four weeks after you left and for your new home from the day you move in. For example, you might rent from a private landlord and have a contract saying you have to pay rent until March. If, because of violence, you moved out into a council house in another town in January, the housing benefit would only cover you on the old house into February.

If you rent a house and move out to somewhere else on a temporary basis until you can get a tenancy transfer to another house, you can get housing benefit for only four weeks on your old house, but can get it on your new one from when you move in. So, if you live in a council house and have your abuser coming around every night beating on the front door until he gets in, the council may agree to transfer you to a safer house once one becomes free. In the meantime you can move into a refuge, and you will get housing benefit for this. You may also get it for the old council house for four weeks. However, if it takes longer than four weeks for you to get a transfer of tenancy, the extra time will not be covered.

Other benefits

There are many other benefits available which cannot be dealt with here. These include council tax benefit, community care grants for families under exceptional stress (which can include domestic violence), free prescriptions and dental treatment, and free school meals. To find out exactly what you are entitled to, seek advice from your local social security office, Citizens' Advice Bureau or a helper at Women's Aid. Solicitors who handle welfare benefits will be able to give you free advice on this area under the legal advice and assistance scheme if you have a low income.

The National Society for the Prevention of Cruelty to Children (NSPCC)

The NSPCC is renowned for its protection of children who are being abused either physically, emotionally or sexually. The society recognizes that this can occur in the context of domestic violence and will be able to offer services to children caught in the crossfire of adult violence. In Liverpool a fairly new group for children who have witnessed domestic violence has been set up. The purpose of the group is to allow children to talk about their experience, and to express their feelings by the use of conversation and workbooks. The workers often find that the children's own behaviour has been affected by the family violence, and so half of the weekly sessions are devoted to play in which workers can help the children to normalize their own behaviour. Contact the national office to see if a similar service exists near you.

A national service for children is the NSPCC helpline. This is a free 24-hour service which provides counselling, information and advice to anyone concerned about a child at risk of abuse. Children can ring themselves, or a parent or other adult who is concerned about the effect of domestic violence on a child can call on their behalf.

The Save the Children Fund

Although this organization is best known for its activities in helping children in developing countries, it also has functions in this country. Its projects often include working with women who have suffered from domestic violence. For example, a project called Lifechance in Oxford is running a women's group called Zcorpio, offering aftercare support for women leaving refuges. They also give help to other agencies who assist victims. Again, for details of services in your area, contact their head office.

Mothers Apart from Their Children (MATCH)

Unfortunately, some women find themselves separated from their children as a result of domestic violence. It may have been the mother's conscious choice not to take her children into refuge accommodation, or older children may have chosen not to accompany her. Other women may have lost a court battle to have their children (see Chapter 7 for more on this topic).

MATCH is a self-help support network for all mothers separated from their children. They offer:

'unconditional and non-judgmental understanding,

support and friendship'
a quarterly newsletter containing useful information and
  shared experiences
informal meetings
a confidential list of members to contact
recommendations on solicitors, counsellors and other
  organizations.

Families Need Fathers (FNF)

Despite its title, FNF states that it is 'the principal society providing advice on children's issues for separated and divorced parents, including unmarried parents, of either sex'. Their purpose is to facilitate continued contact with both parents, but they are opposed to all forms of child abuse.

Victim Support

Victim Support is a national charity helping all crime victims. Assault on a wife or an intimate partner is a criminal offence and Victim Support includes victims of domestic violence in its work. Its general work is to offer emotional support, practical help and information to people suffering from crimes. In addition, in the case of domestic violence they are keen to work with other agencies to ensure the best use of resources, and train their workers to deal with such cases. Victim Support can also offer specific support to victims who are to be witnesses in a criminal prosecution, and specialist help for victims of rape and sexual assault. There are local groups in every area—for more details contact the head office. As well as accepting victims who come direct to Victim Support, they will also help women who are referred from other agencies.

Churches

The church is in essence a collection of people, and therefore its response can depend on the level of understanding of the members in a particular church. However, the message of Christianity is a practical one. The Bible teaches about helping those who are in need, sheltering those who are homeless and soothing those who are hurting. Many churches, therefore, will help a victim of domestic violence if they are approached. The level of help will perhaps not be as organized as that given by a national organization but it will be a personal one. Ministers and many church members are used to talking to people with personal difficulties and will be willing to spend time with a victim who needs to talk about her situation and receive support and friendship. The church also has a powerful message of renewal and recovery which some victims may find helpful. This is covered further in Chapter 8.

If you are wanting to find help close to you the following points may help:

Use the appendices in the back of this book to contact national offices and ask for sources of help near to you.

Once you find one person who can help you, ask them for information about other services. Most agencies have a policy of referral so that a victim gets as much help as possible.

If your abuser checks your phone bill, ring from a phone box so that your calls cannot be traced. If you call from home, make sure the phone does not store the last number dialled. If you think you may leave in an emergency without any cash for phone calls, ask a friend if you can use their phone charge card for emergency calls, and memorize the number.

Consider finding a safe place to keep any leaflets or

letters you may get. Ask a friend or relative whether your solicitor or others can write to you at their address so your abuser will not open your post.

1. Adapted from Child Poverty Action Group, National Welfare Benefits Handbook, 25th edition.

CHAPTER 7

What will happen to my children?

Domestic violence is not just an adult problem—it also concerns children. If a mother is a victim of domestic violence her experiences and decisions do not simply revolve around herself—she has her children to think of too. Earlier chapters discussed how a perpetrator may use the children as a weapon in his abuse of a woman, and how the children's needs may make it difficult for a woman to leave the home. So, how does the violence affect the children themselves—are they too young to understand? Can the violence be hidden from them? Will they just get over it when it all ends?

Sadly the reality is not that simple. Children can be badly affected by domestic violence. Some will be hit and abused themselves. Others may have only an indirect experience of the violence. They can pick up on the tension between the adults and be aware of arguments and fights which take place in the house, even if they are in another room at the time. Others may be present when the violence is happening and may see and hear one parent abusing the other.

The story of Tracey illustrates this well. She was hit by her husband on two consecutive days. On both occasions the assaults took place upstairs while the children were downstairs. She asked an agency for help in getting protection immediately following the second assault, saying she wasn't going to let the situation get worse, as she knew it would. She had two children and she was asked how the children had responded to the violence. She said:

Oh, they don't realize what is going on. They didn't see anything—just him going out and me with a plaster on my head. I told them I'd had an accident. Matthew knows Daddy and I are going to split up, but Lizzie doesn't understand. She is disabled, so she is a bit behind for her age anyway.

Just a few days later she called into the reception area of the agency to drop a document off. The worker dealing with her happened to walk through at the time and stopped to greet her. Suddenly Lizzie, who was in her buggy, asked:

Mummy—are we seeing this lady because Daddy hit you?

The next time she went to talk about her problems she admitted that Matthew, who was now seven, would not go upstairs on his own even though his father was no longer in the house, and that he had become very 'clingy' to his mother.

Whatever their involvement in the situation, domestic violence can have a lasting and detrimental effect on children. In 1994 the first survey on the effects of domestic violence in Britain was published by NCH Action for Children. The results show that children are just as much victims as the adults involved.

The report found that 'in the short term children may be fearful, withdrawn, anxious, aggressive and confused and suffer from disturbed sleep, difficulties at school and problems in making friends'. The survey involved one hundred and eight women, who had two hundred and forty-six children living with them. The following statistics from that survey show how common these short-term effects on children really are:

91% of women believed that their children were affected in the short term

72% said that their children had been frightened

48% said that their children had become withdrawn

34% said that their children had developed bed-wetting problems

31% said that their children had developed problems at school.

The survey also found that children did not get over the effects of domestic violence in the short term—they suffered long-term consequences also:

86% of mothers thought that their children had been affected in the long term

33% thought that their children had become violent and aggressive and harder to control

29% of mothers thought that their children remained resentful and embittered

31% said that their children lacked self-esteem

24% thought that their children had problems trusting people and forming relationships.[1]

Domestic violence destroys the secure environment of the family in which children find their comfort and their identity. They are given skewed ideas of the way in which adults should relate to one another. They may feel split loyalties between their parents—they may love their father but at the same time hate him for hurting their mother. They may feel that they do not want to lose their relationship with their father but that the relationship they are seeking to maintain is less than satisfactory.

One seven-year-old child who took part in an interview with a researcher said:

At my Dad's I wet my knickers by accident and Daddy hit me. I felt scared and unhappy. Sometimes I did not want to see my Dad. I haven't seen my Dad for six weeks now; I feel unhappy because I haven't seen him... I think no one should do domestic violence ever, even in heaven, because if you go to war you could get hurt or end up dead yourself. [2]

They may not have a full understanding of the situation and

may harbour unrealistic fears or hopes which affect their emotional development. A child in the NCH survey said:

I've always got that picture of my Mother in the back of my mind being beaten up and I think oh, all men are like that, that's going to happen to me.

On the other hand, I once dealt with a lady who was going through a bitter and protracted divorce after her husband was violent towards her. The proceedings had been going on for some time when her child said to the childminder:

I wish this divorce was done soon so Mummy and Daddy can live together again and Daddy will be good this time.

Thus, in making decisions about how to deal with the violence and whether or not to leave the home, a victim should not underestimate the effect of remaining in a violent relationship on the children. The children may also suffer in other ways from the breakdown of the relationship—they may have to move school, live on a lower income and so on. A victim has a difficult balancing act to perform in deciding what is in the best interests of the children.

Some victims are hindered in doing this by a lack of knowledge about their legal rights in relation to the children. Perhaps an abuser has constantly told his victim that the children would be taken into care if she ever told anyone about his violence. Or he may tell her that if she leaves she will be classed as an unfit mother and he will be able to keep the children. So what is the true position?

Will my children be taken into care?

A care order is a court order which gives the local authority parental responsibility for the child concerned. Parental responsibility is defined in law as, 'all the rights, duties, powers, responsibilities and authority which by law a parent of a child has in relation to a child and his property'.[3]

When a child is in care a parent keeps the responsibility for the child but cannot use it in a way which is incompatible with the care order. This means that where a child is in care the local authority can say where the children live—for example, with the parents, with foster parents, or in a children's home.

To take a child into care the local authority first has a case conference about the child. This is a meeting of people of different professions, all of whom are involved with the child—for example, the school, social workers, health care workers and so on. The parents also attend a case conference. If, after the meeting, the local authority believes that the child should be placed in its care it must apply to a court for a care order. The procedure can take a while before a final decision is made. While the court is deciding and gathering all the evidence it needs it can make an 'interim care order'—a temporary care order which will last for only about a month at a time and is continually reviewed.

So, can the local authority take a child into care just because they find out that there is domestic violence in the family? Or will they make an application just because a victim seeks help or takes the children out of their usual home for their own safety? What the local authority must prove is that 'the child is suffering, or is likely to suffer significant harm; and that the harm, or the likelihood of harm, is attributable to the care given to the child, or likely to be given to him if the order were not made, not being what it would be reasonable to expect a parent to give to him; or the child's being beyond parental control'.[4]

What does the law mean by harm to the child? It is fairly obvious that physical harm such as sexual abuse or assault on the child is included. However, harm can also be emotional or psychological ill-treatment. Harm also means anything which impairs the child's health or normal development. The harm must be significant. This means not just minor problems, unless they are likely to have serious and long-lasting effects on a child.

It is impossible in a book of this length to explain all about care orders, but a few points can be made as to how they relate to situations of domestic violence. Clearly, domestic violence can put a child at risk. It could well be that they are being physically harmed by the use of direct violence against them. Or perhaps the abuser does not think twice about striking the mother while a baby is in her arms, or about throwing items of furniture around the room in the presence of his children. However, harm can also be emotional. There is an increasing understanding of the emotional effects of domestic violence on children. If a child is being emotionally harmed by the violence this could be grounds for a care order, even if there is no physical harm to the child. This is not to say that in every case of domestic violence where the parents stay together the children will be taken into care.

If a woman takes the children out of the violence to remove them from the risk of harm, that cannot be grounds for a care order unless by taking them away she causes them harm in another way. A parent who takes her children to a refuge or who moves them to another house or a different school is not, just by those acts, harming the children. A move may distress a child but lots of parents move their children for all sorts of reasons and that is not grounds for a care order.

Victims who fear their children may be taken into care may be helped by remembering the following points:

Taking the children out of a violent situation is not harming them or putting them at risk of future harm. Indeed, colluding with a partner to keep them in a violent relationship where they are at risk of harm may result in them being taken into care if the situation is severe enough to warrant this.

Not every family that suffers domestic violence has the children taken into care. This is a remedy of last

resort reserved for the most serious of family problems. In any event it is only recently that people have really started to consider that children can suffer emotional harm from domestic violence between their parents. A local authority and the courts will prefer to support the abused parent first.

A victim should not be afraid to admit that she is being abused because of a fear that her children will be taken into care. Speaking out is the first step in getting the help which will protect the children and herself from further harm. That may mean leaving the home or it may mean obtaining help for the family as a whole. Other chapters in this book give some ideas of the type of help available.

An alternative to a care order is a 'supervision order'. This is a court order which appoints a supervisor whose duty it is to advise, assist and befriend the child. The parents in this case retain full parental responsibility. The test is the same as for a care order.

Another type of court order is a 'family assistance order'. This can be made in exceptional circumstances where the family would benefit from a probation officer or a social worker being made available to advise and assist or befriend any person named in the order. Such an order could be made where a victim is struggling as a result of the violence and needs some formal help to rebuild her life and those of the children, but where the court does not see the need for the children to be taken into care.

A book like this cannot deal with all the law on care and supervision orders. If you are worried that you may have your children taken off you, you should go and see a solicitor or a Citizens' Advice Bureau to find out how the law applies to your situation.

What if we cannot agree about the children between us?

Again, a victim of domestic violence may be afraid that if she seeks to leave the relationship the courts will order that the children should live with the violent partner. Indeed, an abuser may deliberately plant this possibility in the mind of his victim as part of the abuse. So, if a relationship ends, how do the courts decide who has the children living with them? What about the other person—can they still see the children? Again, this book cannot give a detailed explanation of the law, but the following basic explanations may help if you are worried about this.

The law in this area is now mostly governed by the Children Act 1989. In this act there is a principle that if there is agreement between the parties then no court orders will be made unless, for some reason, it is better for the children that there is an order. So, on divorce, the court will not automatically decide who the children live with—they will at first leave it to the parents to see if they can agree.

If the parents cannot agree, then either partner can apply to the court for one or more of several relevant orders. The two most common are:

residence order. This is an order stating with whom a child should live. This replaces what used to be known as 'custody'.

contact order. This is an order requiring the person with whom the child lives to allow the child to have contact with the person named in the order. This used to be called 'access'.

The courts generally see contact as being the right of the child rather than the parent. They consider that children have rights to know their parents no matter what difficulties have occurred between their mother and father. Having said that, the courts will not put a child at risk during contact sessions. Parents will be expected to encourage and facilitate any contact which the court sees appropriate. However, if it is clear that a child cannot cope with a certain form of contact, the court will be reluctant to force him or her to do something which may be emotionally harmful.

There are several different forms of contact order:

staying contact, where a child stays overnight for one or more nights with the other parent

visiting contact, where a child spends time with the other parent but does not sleep over at their house

indirect contact, where there is contact by letters or phone calls but the child does not come face to face with the other person

supervised contact, where the court thinks the child would be at risk if left alone with the other parent. One or more supervisors are named, one of whom must be present throughout contact sessions to make sure the child is protected. A supervisor is often a family member or a mutual friend

no contact, where in absolutely extreme cases the court orders that one parent should not have contact with the child.

Contact orders can combine one or more of these orders. For example, a father who lives a long distance away may have staying contact one weekend in four, but write to the children and phone them weekly. Another father may have the children for the whole weekend one week but the next week only see them for a few hours one evening, so that both parents get to spend weekends with the children.

Contact can be defined, with the order specifying precisely when and where contact will take place each time. Or else it can be left to the parents to agree as time goes on. Again it could be a combination of both. For example, the order may state that the father sees the children every Sunday, for two weeks in the summer and for a week at Easter and Christmas (dates to be agreed), as well as such other contact as may be agreed.

The court can also place a condition on a contact order if it feels it is necessary. So it could be a condition of contact that the children are not taken to a pub, or that a third person is not allowed to join in contact.

What will happen if I take court proceedings?

The court procedure is relatively simple. Some cases settle early on, while others have to go to a full hearing. The following stories illustrate how the system can work.

Jackie left her husband Tom and took her two children to live with her mother. Tom had been violent to her and she found the breakdown of the relationship very hard to cope with. She did not want any contact with him at all and refused him contact with the children. Tom saw his solicitor, who advised him to apply to the court for a contact order. He was on a low income, so the first step was to apply for legal aid. After a month or so the solicitor wrote to Tom to say that he had been granted a legal aid certificate. The next step was for Tom to sign the application forms. His solicitor filled them all in for him, and once Tom had popped into the office to sign them, his solicitor posted them to the local court.

Within a few days, the forms were returned with a notice saying that there would be a short hearing of fifteen minutes in five weeks' time. Tom's solicitors sent a copy of the court papers to Jackie. She took them to her own solicitor, who filled in the reply form for her and also got a legal aid certificate for Jackie so that she could be represented at the hearing.

The hearing day arrived and Jackie was very nervous but wanted things to be as amicable as possible. Her solicitor walked round to the court with her and found her a private room where they could wait. A court welfare officer was on duty at court and both Tom and Jackie were asked if they would speak to him. Jackie was unsure at first. Her solicitor explained that she would not be left alone with her violent partner and that the welfare officer would try to help them reach an agreement. Jackie was told there was no pressure on her to agree to anything but that it was worth trying to talk, to avoid a court hearing. She therefore agreed to speak with her husband and the welfare officer.

After about a quarter of an hour they all re-emerged and Jackie was able to tell her solicitor that they had reached an agreement. She acknowledged now that her husband had never been violent to the children and that they should keep in touch with their father. It had been agreed that Tom would collect the children from her mother every Saturday and that she need not see him. The solicitors then took them in to a judge, who put the agreement into a court order in a short, five-minute hearing.

Riva's case started in the same way but took a different turn. Riva's husband Jonathan had not been violent to her. However, he had left her for a much younger woman in a way which she found devastating. Their cultural community was a tight-knit one and she felt humiliated. Her husband forced her, by his crass behaviour, to leave the matrimonial home, which was worth over £350,000. Riva had to take her three children to live in a two-bedroom flat, rented at a reduced rent from a family friend. He left her with a much reduced lifestyle and close to an emotional breakdown. The children suffered badly in this, especially the older two who were just in their teens and were highly sensitive and intelligent children. All three were adamant that they did not want to see their father. Riva saw how upset they were and refused to push them into it, although she made it clear it was possible for them to change their minds.

Jonathan made an application for contact in the same way as Tom. He was a professional man and did not qualify for legal aid. However, Riva was assessed on her own income and did get legal aid, although she had to pay a contribution. The conciliation meeting with the welfare officer was a disaster. Riva did not feel she could bear to be in the same room as Jonathan, so the court welfare officer agreed to speak to them in different rooms and move between them. Even so, it was impossible to reach an agreement. Riva felt that Jonathan was simply ignoring the children's wishes and blaming her for the situation he had caused.

So, the parties went before a district judge with their lawyers. The judge ordered that Riva and Jonathan should both file statements of their evidence. He ordered that a court welfare officer should prepare a report in twelve weeks' time and that there would be a full hearing before a more senior judge in fourteen weeks' time.

The court welfare officer set about writing her report. She spoke to both the adults and also to the children on several occasions. She made sure that she knew the real reasons for the children's attitudes, being concerned in case Riva was 'poisoning their minds' or putting pressure on them. Her report concluded that the children were genuinely distressed and needed time to get used to the breakdown of their parents' marriage. She said that they could not cope at the present time with face-to-face contact.

At the final hearing, both the parents had a barrister as well as a solicitor with them. Attempts were made to settle the matter—Riva's lawyers asked Jonathan to accept the report's recommendations. If he had, an order could have been made by consent just as in Tom and Jackie's case. However, he wanted to challenge the report—he still felt Riva was to blame.

There was therefore a hearing which lasted a few hours. Both Riva and Jonathan gave evidence about how the marriage ended and, more importantly, about the children and how they felt. The court welfare officer also came to court and was asked more about her report. In the end the judge said that, in this case, he believed that the distress of the children was genuine and that direct contact would harm them at this stage. Jonathan was given permission to write to the children once every three weeks and Riva promised to encourage the children to respond. Usually a decision on contact is a final one, but in this case the judge said that there should be a review in six months' time and a new report by the welfare officer. When the situation was reviewed the children felt the same way, so a final order was made with the proviso that if the children requested direct contact it would be allowed.

Both these cases involved contact, but the procedure is the same for cases where one parent is asking for a residence order. All cases involving children will turn on the individual circumstances, but there is a list of things which judges must take into account. Thinking about this list is how they decide the case. They must consider:

the welfare of the child. This is always the paramount consideration. What is best for the child is the most important thing, not what either adult wants

the ascertainable wishes and feelings of the child concerned, considered in the light of his or her age and understanding. The child will not go to court—as in Riva's case, the court welfare officer will report on this and the parents can give their views

the child's physical and emotional needs

the likely effect on the child of any change in circumstances. In some cases a change can be good, such as when a child is removed from a harmful family environment

the child's age, sex, background and any other characteristics which the court considers relevant

any harm which the child has suffered or is at risk of suffering

how capable each of the parents, and any other relevant person, is of meeting the child's needs.

Obviously, where domestic violence is an issue the court will consider the risks of the child being left with a violent parent. Emotional and physical security are more important than any material comforts which may be available to a child living with an abusive parent. The court will always take care to make a decision which is in the best interests of the child.

Scottish law

As we saw in Chapter 5, Scotland has a slightly different legal system to England and Wales where the above information applies. However, in this area many of the same principles apply. Different terms are used in Scotland. There, residence is still called 'custody' and parental responsibility is 'guardianship'. Contact is referred to as 'access', but the different forms of contact described above also apply to access. The courts have similar checklists to consider and will still make a decision on what is in the best interests of the children.

In conclusion then, victims should remember:

Seeking to stop or escape the violence need not put your children at risk. Indeed, it is usually a beneficial step for them.

The courts will take into account a history of domestic violence when deciding what is best for the children. They will not put them at risk of further abuse.

Each situation is different and if you are worried about your children you should seek legal advice. Many firms will give a free short initial interview and many parents qualify for legal aid to take the case to court.

1. NCH Action For Children, The Hidden Victims, 1994
2. 'Childright', Children's Legal Centre, March 1995
3. Children Act 1989 s 3 (1)
4. Children Act 1989 s 31 (2)

CHAPTER 8

From victim to survivor

Domestic violence is a life-altering experience. The previous chapters have shown in stark reality how it can have a devastating effect on the lives of victims. It can alter personalities, rip families apart and wreak havoc on the financial and emotional security of all those involved. In so many cases the suffering goes on for years before the secret comes out, or until the victim is in a position to be able to seek help. In that time the effects of domestic violence on the victim are reinforced and compounded. Leaving the relationship or getting a court order does not solve the problem overnight. Even for a woman who is lucky enough to be able to stay in the matrimonial home with sufficient money to feed and clothe her children, there will still be considerable problems to face.

Domestic violence is about psychological control, degradation and humiliation as much as—some would say more than—the physical injuries. The pain within a victim's heart can remain long after broken bones have healed and the scars have faded. We have seen how children's development can be affected by the violence long after the abuser has been removed from their lives.

Crisis intervention, providing emergency accommodation and immediate financial provision, is akin to taking a car accident victim to the emergency department of a hospital. That kind of immediate treatment is vital if the victim is to survive. However, it is only the start of the treatment. Thereafter, the car accident victim will need recuperation and physiotherapy. She will need, perhaps, to relearn some of the basic skills of life which others take for granted. She will have to learn to walk again—first with crutches and then unassisted as she gains strength. As time goes on, her dependency will diminish and she will regain independence and an ability to live a full life. She may always have scars to remind her of the past, but these need not diminish her capacity to live life to the full in the future.

In a way it is the same for the victim of domestic violence. The first stages of escaping from the violence and setting up again in a place of safety—be that a permanent new home, a temporary refuge or in one's own home with a court order for protection—is akin to the treatment by the paramedics and the emergency team in the hospital. After that, there must be time for healing and for adjustment to a new non-violent life. At first the victim will need practical help and emotional support—the 'crutches'—while she learns to walk anew. However, in time, a victim may become independent and able to live a fulfilled life on her own. There may always be reminders of her old life. For example, the children may still have contact with the abuser, or she may always associate a certain song with a beating she received while it was on the radio. However, in time, a victim will be able to live a new life undiminished by her old experiences.

In other words, an abused person will turn from being a victim and become a survivor.

There is some debate among those working in the area of domestic violence as to whether the term 'victim' should ever be used for those who are experiencing domestic violence. The argument against it is that use of the word can continue to identify the abused person in the negative, as a downtrodden person with no hope. The word 'survivor' implies hope and gives positive messages. In this book the two terms have deliberately been used in two separate contexts. The term 'victim' has been used for women who are continuing to suffer domestic violence. This is not to say that those women have not in their own way shown a capacity for survival. For some, just to stay alive in the face of the violence is survival at its most basic. For others, to be able to say that they have brought their children up well without succumbing to the tempting, numbing effects of alcohol or drugs is to survive. However, I have reserved the term 'survivor' to refer to those women who, having left the violence, have rebuilt their lives out of the rubble of their broken relationship and have moved into a new stage of their lives. The term 'survivor' has been chosen to give the message that an abused person can hope for more than just coping. She can look to a brighter future.

That is not to gloss over the difficulties faced by victims of domestic violence in attempting to rebuild their lives. There are still so often problems of poverty, loneliness, the stress of being a single parent, and conflicting emotions to deal with. It can take time to come out the other side. However, it is possible to move from being a victim to being a survivor.

Each victim/survivor is a unique individual and there are dangers in trying to lump everyone together and seeking to prescribe the same generic 'medicine' for everyone. However, this chapter offers some suggestions for rebuilding lives after violence which have worked for others and may work for you too.

Counselling

Counselling is commonly offered as a part of the package offered to women seeking help from Women's Aid, and is also available from other sources. So what is counselling—what does it have to offer?

Counselling is not about advice, not about someone else living your life for you and is not about psychiatric treatment or hypnotherapy. So what is it? In fact, counselling is not easy to define. The counsellor John Rowan said that for clients at a certain stage it is 'about adjustment. It will be about regaining our roles, regaining our respect, regaining our balance'.[1]

Open Door Counselling, a Liverpool agency, described it to me as being about helping people to help themselves, about helping people to deal with their worlds and to develop their own living skills. They described their role as making a flat picture into a hologram for their client.

Counselling can be about empowering. It can help a client to see the skills which she does have and the strengths she does possess. It helps her to see the positive and not the negative. A counsellor's job is to make a client independent—to encourage her to step out on her own.

So how is this achieved? Essentially a counsellor will get the client to talk about whatever has brought her there. She will listen and plant seeds in the victim's mind to enable her to begin to think through her own problems. For example, a client may say:

'I just don't know where to turn next.'

A counsellor might respond:

'Have you thought about your family? Are they a possibility?'

In this way, the client may come to realize that there are avenues open to her which she had not thought of before. A counsellor will not programme a client into taking a certain route in her life, as if she were an aeroplane on automatic pilot. However, she can help her unfold a map so that she can see all the roads which are open to her.

There are many different techniques in counselling and it is beyond the scope of this book to go into them in detail. However, the following are examples of how a counsellor may work with you.

Cognitive process counselling

A victim may look at a certain event and see the consequences she believes will follow. A counsellor can get her to look at the event differently and change her thought processes to allow for the possibility of a different outcome.

Neurolinguistic programming
or re-framing

This is counselling aimed at changing how you look at a situation and adding in other aspects to alter the picture. For example, take a woman who has been kept in isolation and has now left the violent home, but feels useless and unable to support herself. She was married at sixteen and has been effectively housebound until now. She looks at her lack of formal training and education and cannot see what she can do with her new life. With counselling, that can be turned around so that she can see the skills she has developed in her situation. She may have childcare skills, expertise at housekeeping and home accounts or cooking skills. She will have a personal experience which could equip her to work with other victims.

Personal growth counselling

This type of counselling is about knowing yourself better—about understanding your own beliefs, reactions, the effect of your upbringing and so on. This can include looking at violent behaviour, or responses to violence which have been learned from someone else. It can sometimes be useful for victims of domestic violence to understand why they react the way they do. This may be the first step to change. A victim may need to know where she is starting from so that she knows where she can go next.

For example, a woman may feel that she ought to stay in the violent home. With counselling she may identify that the main reason she feels she ought to do this is because her mother's influence on her is very strong and her mother believes in marriage being for life. She can then go on to explore whether that is what she herself believes. If it is, she can go on to think about how she can best deal with the violence from within the marriage. If it is not, then she may feel more able to move away.

Religious or cultural background counselling

Similar processes can take place if the person being counselled has been heavily influenced by a particular culture or religion. A counsellor can help a client to think about the issues in her life in the context of her cultural or religious influences. She can guide the client to consider more deeply the teachings which she had perhaps simply accepted without thought. A counsellor will help a client work through her problems within the constraints which she herself accepts and not those which have been imposed upon her.

For example, a client could be an Asian woman who has been brought up to believe that women should not work outside the home and should behave in a traditionally demure way. If, on looking at them closely, she accepts these teachings as valid then she may move on to exploring the possibility of specialist refuges. If not, then she will perhaps come to understand how that isolation of women had in fact been part of her abuse and she will be much freer to take action to get herself out of the violence.

Coping mechanisms

Counselling can show victims how to cope with specific issues which are causing them stress, such as debt, alcohol dependency or loneliness.

Confidentiality

Legally a counsellor cannot guarantee total confidentiality in the same way that a solicitor can. However, a counsellor should establish from the start what she can keep confidential and what she cannot. There will be very few occasions on which a counsellor will choose to reveal information which you divulge—one may be if you have said that you will harm a child, for example. However, the issue of confidentiality should be discussed at the beginning of a counselling relationship so you know where you stand.

Where can I get counselling?

private agencies—you can find them by recommendation, from the Yellow Pages, or from the British Association for Counselling, whose address appears in Appendix 1

Women's Aid groups (see Appendix 1)

doctors—increasingly, doctors are realizing that if problems can be solved or alleviated by counselling, their patients are less likely to have stress-related illnesses which require treatment on the NHS. Therefore, some doctors are now offering counselling in the surgery for those patients whom they think are in need. However, this can be limited to a set number of weeks, which is not always enough for each patient's needs. Fundholding GPs can choose to use some of their funds to pay for counselling from a private agency. It is worth consulting your GP to see if he or she has such a provision.

Befriending

It is perhaps obvious that an antidote to the problems of isolation resulting from domestic violence is befriending. This can be found on a one-to-one basis, or in self-help groups such as those run by Women's Aid and similar groups, where people with similar needs or interests gather together to talk and support each other. The advantage of befriending is that it provides company and mutual support as well as practical help. For example, for single parents, Mother and Toddler groups can give welcome adult conversation as well as putting mothers in touch with people who can act as babysitters in a rota system. Women joining domestic violence self-help groups can find that being able to share their experiences with others who have gone through the same things is beneficial. Not only is being able to disclose what has had to remain secret cathartic, but many women find it healing to learn that they are not alone in their experiences, that they are not a freak or abnormal, but are one of many women in the same position.

Positive action

Positive action is about actively seeking to rebuild a damaged life. Domestic violence demeans victims. It takes away their choice and freedom. It removes the opportunities for self-betterment.

It can help for would-be survivors to set goals, either with others or alone, to achieve something which they could not do while they were being abused. For some victims, this could be a large goal:

Terri went to work with a women's group and helped them set up a new refuge.

Susan went back to college and did foundation exams, A levels and finally a degree course.

Karen used her divorce settlement to set up her own business.

For others, their goals may seem small in comparison but in reality represent just as much progress in the context of their own lives:

Ayeesha had been unable to leave her home much. She set a goal of exploring a different area of her city each month.

Maggie had never been allowed a say in the decor of the

house. Once she was alone, she redecorated each room as she could afford it.

Denise cut the hair her husband liked long, and bought make-up in a different shade.

Ellen had been kept without access to money of her own, and when she left she found it difficult to cope with being in control of her own finances. When it was pointed out to her that she had lost the natural instinct to spend on impulse, she began to set aside a small amount of money each week and allowed herself 'mad money'. In this way she was able to treat herself to small items—a chocolate bar here, a lipstick there—which for her was a way of rebuilding her own self-esteem.

Hope and trust

It is easy and understandable for victims either to swear they will never enter another relationship again or else to begin a relationship with another abusive man. Many women find fulfilment and happiness in leading new single lives. Others long for true love. Not all potential partners are abusive and for those lucky enough to meet a loving and caring partner, that new relationship can actually help a victim get over the previous abuse. One woman sent me an e-mail from the USA, talking about how she has become a survivor. At the end she said simply:

My current husband is part of the reason I am still alive. I know that and appreciate it, whilst at the same time realizing that perhaps I am the reason he is still here too.

To go from an abusive relationship to such a mutual sharing and dependency of equals is a sign of survivorship.

Spiritual hope and trust

For those victims who have a religious belief or are searching for some meaning in their lives, spiritual messages can have a great healing effect. The Christian message is one of healing and hope for those who are hurting. Throughout the Bible the message is that situations can be turned about and good made out of bad. The Bible speaks about a loving God who cares and tends gently to those who come to him in need. It talks about how he nurtures them and gives them strength to go on. This message is powerfully expressed by the words of one of the Old Testament prophets:

Give strength to hands that are tired and to knees that tremble with weakness. Tell everyone who is discouraged, 'Be strong and don't be afraid! God is coming to your rescue'... Streams of water will flow through the desert; the burning sand will become a lake, and dry land will be filled with springs. Where jackals used to live, marsh grass and reeds will grow.[2]

Victims with a belief in God may prefer to seek Christian counselling as an alternative to secular counselling. Christian counsellors will use many of the practical techniques used by secular counsellors. However, they will bring an added dimension to the counselling. They will counsel with the intention of leading the client closer to God, to allow her to enjoy the healing which comes from a relationship with God and to stimulate her to choose courses of action which are in accord with biblical standards. A Christian counsellor will seek to encourage spiritual growth in a client as well as fostering emotional development.

Christian counsellors local to you may be found through a local church, or through the Association of Christian Counsellors (see Appendix 1). Some Christian counsellors will be informally trained within the church—others will be professional counsellors who also practise their Christian faith.

Help for children

Children too need help in becoming survivors of violence. They can have their own problems in overcoming the effects of the abuse. They are not always considered to be victims by the adults dealing with the child's mother, and may therefore not be given help. They are not always able to verbalize their feelings, and they may be reluctant to tell about their experiences for several reasons:

shame
fear of retaliation from their abuser
embarrassment
**they may wish to protect their mother from more
  distress and pain**
**they may not wish to be any different from the other
  children they know**
they may fear not being believed.

Nevertheless, children who have lived in a home with domestic violence generally have feelings with which they find it hard to cope. They may feel fear, anger, guilt, confusion, terror, loneliness, sadness, happiness, relief and so on. Mixed emotions such as these are tough for an adult to cope with. For a child whose understanding and coping skills are not yet fully developed it can be doubly hard.

In Women's Aid a high priority is placed on child work. It is often underfunded, but help is available. Where funds allow, local groups may have a children's worker for the children in the refuge. If they have the money, they may also work with children who remain in a violent home or who have left the refuge but still need support. Other agencies mentioned in Chapter 6 can also help children become survivors.

A publication by Scottish Women's Aid entitled *Children— Equality and Respect* (1994) indicates that children's workers can fulfil a number of roles:

supporting the children

acting as a children's advocate, speaking up for their
    concerns, needs and rights

enabling the children to talk about their feelings

allowing the children to work out their anger

giving the children fun on trips out or play sessions

liaising with other agencies to ensure that the best
    services are provided for children

allowing the children to build up confidence and trust
    in them so they have someone to confide in

encouraging the children to support each other by
    sharing their experiences and in play

helping the children gain self-esteem

helping children realize that the violence is not their
    fault.

As in adult counselling there are various techniques which
can be used to help children become survivors. For example:

Art therapy

This allows children to express themselves in art or model-
making when they do not have the words to tell what they feel.
The art can then be interpreted with the child to reveal what lies
beneath. For example, it is common for children who have been
abused to depict themselves without arms and legs, which
reflects their feelings of powerlessness. Children who have
experienced violence often draw pictures of monsters being
killed, indicating that they wish the violence to stop.

Play therapy

Various forms of play can be used for specific purposes. Play can
be used to normalize children's behaviour so that overly
aggressive or submissive tendencies are reduced.

The effects of domestic violence should not be underestimated. The emotional effects may last longer than the physical signs. It is not simply a question of leaving the abuser and immediately living happily ever after.

Victims have the right to take their time to get over the experience. They deserve long-term understanding and support without a time limit. No shame should be felt in continuing to use the support services mentioned in this book long after the actual abuse has ceased.

It is possible to survive—and not merely to endure life, but to build a new life which is fulfilled and contented. It is possible to exchange feelings of fear for security, uselessness for self-confidence and despair for hope. Other people have walked this path and you can too.

1. Counselling February 1995, p. 12
2. Isaiah 35:3-7

CHAPTER 9

Looking to a better future

Karen found herself in a dilemma. Her husband was violent to her on a regular basis and she felt that she could no longer live in constant fear of his temper. On the other hand, she believed that marriage was a commitment for life. She looked back to their wedding and remembered how much love for her husband she had felt at that time. She felt that the violence was destroying that love and she desperately wanted it back. However, her husband's violence seemed to be a descending spiral—the longer she stayed, the worse it would get. On the other hand, if she left that would destroy the relationship once and for all.

Fortunately for women in Karen's position, living in fear or leaving are not always the only options. A third solution is counselling aimed at stopping the violence and rebuilding the marriage. Obviously, this will require the wholehearted commitment of the abuser, since it is primarily his behaviour and attitudes which will have to change for the relationship to be restored. Even while counselling is taking place, the woman may need temporary protection from the violence—counselling is not an overnight solution to a deep-rooted attitude and pattern of behaviour. Nevertheless, counselling is a viable option for some couples. It may take one of two basic forms— either relationship counselling for the couple together, or individual counselling for the abuser.

Couple counselling

Among those working with abusive relationships there are two views. Some feel that domestic violence is solely an issue for the abuser, that he alone is responsible for the state of the relationship and so the solution lies with changes in him alone. Others believe that as a relationship involves two individuals, both of them have a part to play in the healing process. This is not to say that the parties have equal responsibility for the violence—just that having lived in a violent relationship together, both need to play their part in the restoration of the relationship.

The latter view leads to the provision of couple counselling or relationship counselling. This can take place in various combinations of individual counsellors and clients, and two counsellors and clients working together. This type of counselling looks at the individuals themselves and the effect they have on the other person, and how they in turn are affected by their partner. It can look at the communication skills between the couple and helps them develop listening skills and methods of dealing with confrontation in non-violent means.

Couple counselling need not be about looking at how the woman encourages the man or how she is to blame for his behaviour. It need not move away from the principle that the abuser is responsible for his behaviour. However, it can help the couple grow in a non-violent relationship together. For example, let us consider the fictional example of Dave and Kim.

Dave and Kim have a violent relationship which goes back many years. He has promised time and time again to change, but his behaviour always turns violent again. The pattern is generally a period of slow-burning anger in Dave when he is moody, sullen and unpredictable. This explodes into a very violent assault, but immediately afterwards he enters the 'honeymoon period' when he is loving towards her, buys her gifts and showers her with affection.

Couple counselling may help Dave to realize just how deeply the violence affects Kim. By learning how she is made to feel, he can learn that his behaviour is not just a flash in the pan, for which he can apologize, but a deep-seated pattern of abuse. He may also understand that his attitudes about the role of women and the use of violence, which he may have learned from his own father, are not in fact appropriate. He will be supported over time in his attempts to unlearn his usual behaviour and to learn fresh ways of relating to Kim.

In the counselling, Kim will have the opportunity to show Dave just how she is feeling, which can be empowering. She will be able to make sense of the violence by following Dave's own learning process, and will be able to support him. However, she may also begin to realize that the periods of built-up tension are actually the hardest for her. She may come to appreciate that she fears the unpredictability of Dave's moods and the waiting for the inevitable assault more than the violence itself. Perhaps she finds out that to get this period over and done with she sometimes actually provokes the violence, so that the couple can move on to the loving side more quickly.

This is not to say that she is to blame for the violence, or that she causes it. It is just to say that she has developed a coping mechanism to deal with Dave's violence. However, if she continues with that method of coping with the relationship at the same time as Dave is attempting to change his attitude, it may undermine his attempts. That is not to say either that she should not try to protect herself while Dave is working through his problems. However, it may be productive for them both if she can learn to recognize the steps forwards which he has made and begin to trust him and respond to the genuine changes.

Christian couple counselling

As with the individual counselling mentioned in Chapter 8, Christian counselling can add to secular techniques a biblical perspective which may assist those with Christian beliefs. An interesting example of how Christian couple counselling can be effective is the account of the marriage of an adviser to the Archbishop of Canterbury.

It was reported in the press that Canon Michael Green and his wife Rosemary Green had had problems with violence in their marriage. Interestingly, it was Mrs Green who was the perpetrator of the violence. After a particularly difficult year friends encouraged them to seek counselling, which they continued with for a year. Mrs Green has said:

There was this reservoir of anger built up in me from years ago. It was rooted in the fact that my father was killed in a climbing accident in the Himalayas when I was a baby and my mother brought three of us up on her own... I married Michael just a few years after university, not knowing anything about men, and had four children in six years. Then the whole anger exploded. I took it out on Michael and the children.

Of the counselling which followed she said, 'I got rid of all the anger. I got rid of the build-up of the resentment towards my mother, who did the best she could within her limits.' She accepted that she wasn't necessarily right to think that 'because I've been hurt I have a right to be angry'. The time of counselling was for her like 'pushing away a heavy black lid so the Holy Spirit could go deep down into the past hurt and, painful though it was, bring healing'.

When their experience was reported in the press, Canon Green said that their marriage had been 'gloriously sorted out'.[1]

Perpetrator counselling

Again, there are various forms of perpetrator counselling—counselling for the abuser—and the differences between different programmes often reflect the view of domestic violence which is held by those running the programmes. There are four basic types of programme.[2]

Insight model

Basis: This type of programme looks at the man's own character, and the reasons he reacts violently to given situations. It also looks at the man's own levels of frustration or depression and any mental illness from which he may suffer.

Drawbacks: This kind of approach can be a tool to enable the man to change. However, it does not strongly challenge the violence and does not categorize the violence as a social problem. Also, making men aware of their violent propensities alone does not necessarily mean that they will change.

Ventilation model

Basis: This type of counselling discourages the holding in of anger and looks at alternative non-violent ways for the abuser to express his feelings, so that he will not allow built-up tension to explode in aggressive behaviour.

Drawbacks: As we have seen, verbal abuse can be as harmful as physical violence, so to transfer physical expression of tension into a tirade of verbal abuse against the victim is not really a solution.

Cognitive behavioural and psycho-educational model

Basis: Programmes under this heading focus on the violence of the abuser as being a learned behaviour which needs to be unlearned. It teaches anger management techniques.

Drawbacks: An abuser who learns to control his anger without recourse to physical violence may still have a pattern of controlling behaviour. For example, he may still isolate his victim or keep her short of money. Again, this type of counselling individualizes the problem of domestic violence. Also, there is some danger that the victim may be blamed as being the source of the anger in the first place. An abuser who feels that he hits his wife because she is a bad housekeeper may stop hitting her but may still have unrealistic expectations of the role of a wife.

Pro-feminist approach

This is the type of perpetrator counselling which is most accepted by women's groups these days.

Basis: In programmes like this the violence is believed to be just one way of controlling the victim, just one way in which the abuser keeps his power over his partner. The courses do cover communication and assertion skills together with an education in non-violent ways of dealing with tension. However, the courses also focus on challenging the male controlling behaviour and attitudes, and aim at ending all forms of violence.

Programmes such as this tend to draw heavily on the methods developed by the Domestic Abuse Intervention Project in Duluth, Minnesota (see Appendix 2). These courses were primarily developed in the United States but are fast developing here too. Appendix 1 gives the names and numbers of some centres offering this type of counselling.

Another new development is the provision of counselling of

this type within the criminal justice system. If a woman presses criminal charges following an assault by a partner, in some areas therapy can be made available to the abuser through the courts. The idea is not to let the abusers off, but to impose an effective sentence which will really help the victim. The message is that domestic violence is a crime and ought to be punished. After a conviction, the abuser can be sentenced to probation and the court can make it a condition of that probation that he attend a course for the perpetrators of domestic violence.

Some private counsellors would say that you cannot force an abuser to change in this way—he must want to attend the course himself. However, the probation service argues that forcing him to attend a course like this is actually part of the punishment. If it gets hard for him, or if the times are inconvenient, he must still go. For some men, forcing them to face up to their own behaviour is the only way to get them to even think about their violence.

Probation services are also developing such programmes in prisons and for offenders who have been released from prison on licence. An example of this type of programme is that run by the Domestic Violence Probation Project in Edinburgh. This was described by the Assistant Chief Probation Officer of Essex as 'essentially a re-education project designed to change the values, beliefs and behaviours which provide the foundations for the use of violence'.[3]

Liverpool Probation also runs a probation scheme. It is a twenty-week programme, with one session per week being a condition of probation. It aims to provide 'greater protection for women by encouraging perpetrators to take responsibility for their violent behaviour and its consequences, thereby reducing the risk of further violent offending and abusive behaviour towards women'.

The course stresses that the violence is the perpetrator's problem and that it is his responsibility to do something about it. It fosters partnerships with other agencies so that they can stress the far-reaching consequences of domestic violence. For example, the NSPCC come in to talk about the effect on children. The course challenges the abuser's belief systems. For example, he must use his partner's name and not terms like 'the missus' or 'the old woman'. This is to stress that the woman is a person and not an object.

The development of courses such as these means that there is a way forward for an abuser. So often victims of domestic violence have heard their partners promising to change but also claiming that there is plenty of help for the victims but nothing for them. This is no longer the case. It is true that there is still more provision for the victims than the perpetrators. That is probable, because the development of these counselling schemes is still a relatively new thing. There is also a general feeling that while they are a vital service, they should not be paid for at the expense of services offering victims protection and a chance to rebuild their lives. However, funding may be short but there is now no excuse for the abuser who says he cannot find help.

1. The Times, Saturday 8 June 1996, p. 11 and the Daily Express, Saturday 8 June 1996, p. 3.
2. As defined by Gill Hague and Ellen Malos in Domestic Violence—Action for Change (1993).
3. Victim Support one-day conference on domestic violence.

Conclusion

Domestic violence is now a concern which is receiving a lot of attention in society. Across the country, public money is being made available to fund administrators to coordinate services for victims. More money is being spent on training, so that people whose jobs may bring them into contact with victims of domestic violence will know how best to help them. Certain cities have run high-profile advertising campaigns under the banner of 'Zero Tolerance'. The idea of these campaigns is to use TV and other media adverts to get the message across to abusers and victims alike that domestic violence is not acceptable, that there are alternatives.

It is without doubt a good thing that domestic violence as a cause is receiving this attention. However, domestic violence, at its most basic, is not a political issue or a social concern alone— it is about the suffering of individual people, none of whom deserve to live in the shame, pain and humiliation which domestic violence involves.

This book has tried to show victims that they are not just statistics on a government crime survey or unnoticed faces which have joined a throng of hidden victims. Each woman who has lived with domestic violence is an individual with individual needs. The good news is that solutions are available and each individual will be able—with help and courage—to find her own way out of the violence. Some families are able to work through the problems or find that changing circumstances reduce the violence. In the case of Aileen, mentioned in the Introduction, her parents never separated. However, the Second World War meant that employment opportunities for her father improved as the able-bodied men were sent to war. After he got a job the situation, as far as Aileen could tell, became much easier.

Other families are forced to take much more drastic measures. It would give false hope if it was not admitted that some women are forced to flee their homes and to set up new identities and homes in a new area. For them, fear may remain, but a day-to-day freedom can be found. Other families take a middle route, with some form of separation or counselling involved.

This book has given information which shows the various paths available. For a victim still living with the violence or having only recently fled her abuser, it can be difficult to see clearly the path ahead. A book of this nature cannot give a step by step blueprint of what every victim should do in the future. Each victim is an individual and will have her own individual path to freedom to follow. However, there are people who can devote time to a victim and who can help her make the first few steps forward to a new life.

Moving out of a violent relationship can be compared with emigrating to a new country. Indeed, for some women it may seem just as big a step. If you are a victim of domestic violence, imagine you had moved to, say, South Africa or Australia. Looking back, you would be able to see that there was a sequence of steps which you might not have thought important at the time. Before flights were booked and suitcases were packed, there would have been an even earlier time of preparation. The very first step would have been to believe that it was possible for you to emigrate. Without believing that, and without it being a dream you wished to come true, the journey would never have happened.

Then you would have begun some advance planning. You would perhaps have talked to other people who had been to other countries, to see which journey was the best for you personally to make. You may have talked to foreign embassies to get information about visas or job opportunities. You may have spoken to relatives abroad to see if they would help you, or to friends at home to see if they could give you support. Then you would have considered all your options and, eventually, plucked up the courage to make a decision and to book your flight. Of course, after that there would be many practical arrangements. When you got to your new home there would be a period of adjustment and resettlement. At one stage, you would probably have had a list of so many tasks to sort out that you didn't know where to start.

Perhaps you spent many years planning your trip. You might have gathered a lot of information and planned every last detail before you left. Perhaps you waited until your children had finished their schooling. Or perhaps you left in a hurry—maybe your company offered you a post abroad and you had to leave at once. You might have dealt with all the arrangements yourself. Or perhaps the personnel department in your company helped or you used the services of a professional emigration department.

In many ways, leaving a violent relationship is the same. There will be many practical aspects which need to be sorted out. There will be pieces of information you will wish to gather, to make sure you are headed in the right direction. For a victim who has been made so weary and lacking in self-confidence by the violence, the thought of dealing with all that can be off-putting. The important thing to remember is that nothing need stop you taking the first step—that of believing that it is possible to get out of the violence. Once you have done that, you have taken one step which your abuser would not want you to take—and which he has not been able to stop you from taking. It is one small step further just to make one phone call to an agency named in this book. Perhaps the next step for you then is just to think about how you would like your life to be. In this way, with small steps you can get yourself nearer and nearer to your goal. Again, some women will do all this themselves. Others will seek professional help.

The Bible has many stories about people who are facing difficult journeys. One example is a man called Joshua, who was about to lead the people of Israel into the Promised Land. He was standing on the wrong side of a river looking across into the land in which he wanted his people to live. He could see where he wanted to go, but he knew that the journey would not be easy. For a start, they would have to get the people and their belongings across the river. Then they would have to face enemy armies and would have to start again in new places with only their basic provisions. They were weary, having spent forty years wandering around a desert.

Joshua probably felt very scared. Perhaps he wondered whether things would be better on the other side, or whether they should stay in the inhospitable desert because at least they knew that environment. Perhaps he was wondering where his people would get the strength they needed to fight their way into the Promised Land. He would certainly have felt responsible for the people he was going to take with him. In other words, he must have felt just like many victims of domestic violence feel. However, God had a special message for Joshua. It is a message which the Bible repeats in other ways, and which is true not just for Joshua but also for people today facing 'spiritual journeys' like Joshua's. God told Joshua to rely on him and on his word. Then, he said:

'Be strong and courageous. Do not be terrified; do not be discouraged, for the Lord your God will be with you wherever you go' (Joshua 1:9).

This message holds true for victims of domestic violence who feel all alone. God remains with you if you choose to travel with him. In addition, there are people out there who will walk with you to a new life. The first step is there for you to take today—why not take it now?

APPENDIX 1

Sources of Help

Association of Christian Counsellors
173A Wokingham Road
Reading
Berkshire RG6 1LT
Tel: 01734 662207

British Association for Counselling
1 Regent Place
Rugby
Warwickshire CV21 2PJ
Tel: 01788 550899

Childline
2nd Floor
Royal Mail Building
Studd Street
London N1 OQW
Tel: 0171 239 1000

Families Need Fathers (FNF)
Administration Office
134 Curtain Road
London EC2A 3AR
Tel: 0171 613 5060
Information line: 0181 886 0970

Mothers Apart From their Children (MATCH)
c/o BM Problems
London WC1N 3XX

The Men's Centre
(a men's service offering counselling on domestic violence)
Tel: 0171 267 8713

Merseyside Abusive Partner's Project (MAPP)
(based at St Helen's Women's Aid)
Tel: 01744 454290

NCH Action For Children
85 Highbury Park
London N5 1UD
Tel: 0171 226 2033

Newham Asian Women's Project
PO Box 225
London E7 9AA
Tel: 0181 472 0528

Northern Ireland Women's Aid Federation
129 University Street
Belfast B17 1HP
Tel: 01232 249041/249358

NSPCC Child Protection Helpline
Tel: 0800 800 500

National Society for the Prevention of Cruelty to Children
(NSPCC)
National Centre
42 Curtain Road
London EC2A 3NH
Tel: 0171 825 2500

Refuge
PO Box 855
Chiswick
London W4 4JF
Tel: 0181 747 0133
24-hour crisis line: 0181 995 4430

The Save the Children Fund
17 Grove Lane
London SE5 8RD
Tel: 0171 703 5400

Scottish Women's Aid
12 Torpichen Street
Edinburgh EH3 8JQ
Tel: 0131 221 0401

Solas Anois
Irish Women's Domestic Violence Project
Tel: 0181 664 6089

Victim Support National Office
Cranmer House
39 Brixton Road
London SW9 6DZ
Tel: 0171 735 9166

Victim Support Scotland
14 Frederick Street
Edinburgh EH2 2HB
Tel: 0131 225 7779

Victim Support Republic of Ireland
Room 16
29/30 Dane Street
Dublin 2
Tel: 00353 16798673

Welsh Women's Aid National Offices:
12 Cambrian Place
Aberystwyth
Dyfed SY23 1NT
Tel: 01970 612748

26 Wellington Road
Rhly
Clwyd LL18 1BN
Tel: 01745 334767

38/48 Crwys Road
Cardiff CF2 4NN
Tel: 01222 390874

Women's Aid Federation England Ltd
PO Box 391
Bristol BS99 7WS
Tel: 0117 944 4411
National helpline: 0117 963 3542

APPENDIX 2

Sources of Help in the USA

Domestic violence is a worldwide problem and it is impossible to list all the resources available to victims and abusers in other countries. However, this list provides a selection of US resources.

Domestic Abuse Intervention Project
Minnesota Program Development, Inc.
706 West Fourth Street
Duluth, MN 55806
Tel: 218 722 2781
(family violence intervention, focusing on rehabilitation)

Alternatives to Violence
Alternatives Counselling Associates
3703 Long Beach Boulevard, Suite E10
Long Beach, CA 90807
(group and individual counselling for batterers and survivors of domestic violence)

Alternatives to Domestic Violence
Bergen County Department of Human Services
21 Main Street, Room 111
Court Plaza
South Hackensack, NJ 07601
Tel: 201 487 8484
(counselling and education for victims of domestic violence)

Metro Nashville Police Department
8 a.m.–11 p.m.: 880-3000
After 11 p.m.: 862-8600

Coatal Women's Shelter
1333 S. Glenburnie Road
New Bern, NC 2856
Office: 919 638-4509
24-hour crisis line: 919 638-5995

Crossroads
PO Box 993
Fort Collins, CO 80522
Tel: 970/482-3502
(safe house for victims)

Shelter Against Violent Environments
PO Box 8283
Fremont, CA 94537
Tel: 510-794-6056 (9 a.m.-5 p.m.)
24-hour hotline: 510 794 6055

Shelter for South Asian Victims of Domestic Violence
(AASRA), New York
Hotline: 1-800-313-ASRA (2772)
Community Office: 510-505-7503

Men Overcoming Violence (MOVE)
San Francisco
415-777-4496
San Francisco Man Alive Latino Men's Programme
415-552-4801

Hotlines:
Arkansas 1-800-332-4443

Colorado crisis 24-hour hotline: (719) 589-2465
Indiana 1-800-334-7233
LA county 1-800-978-3600
Michigan 1-800-99-NO ABUSE or 1-800-996-6228
Nevada 1-800-992-5757
New Hampshire 1-800-852-3311
New Jersey 1-800-572-7233
New York (English) 1-800-942-6906
New York (Spanish) 1-800-942-6908
North Dakota 1-800-472-2911
Oklahoma 1-800-522-7233
Pennsylvania (eastern) 1-800-642-3150
Texarkana area 1-800-876-4808
Washington 1-800-562-6025
Wisconsin 1-800-333-7233

For a listing of every domestic violence coalition phone
National Resource Centre on:
1 (800) 537 2238

APPENDIX 3

A safety plan

Completing the following plan may help you increase your safety and prepare in advance for possible violence in the future. You may not be able to control your partner's violence but you can plan how best to respond to that violence and how to keep yourself and your children safe.

If you have difficulty in completing this plan consider asking for help from a Women's Aid worker, your counsellor, or a close friend whom you can trust.

This plan has been adapted from one published on the Internet by the Nashville Police Department.

Step one—safety during a violent incident

If my partner is violent to me again I can use some or all of the following strategies:

1. If I decide to leave I will.....................
(Practise how to get out safely. Which doors, windows, stairs or lifts would you use?)

2. I can keep my purse and keys ready and put them in .... so that they will be to hand if I need to leave quickly.

3. I can tell .... about the violence and ask them to call the police if they hear suspicious sounds coming from my house.

4. I can teach my children how to use the telephone to call the police and the ambulance.

5. I will use .... as a code for my children or friends so they know when to call for help.

6. If I have to leave my home I will go to ....
If I cannot go to this place then I will go to .... or
....

7. I can also teach some of these strategies to some or all of my children.

8. When I expect that there is going to be violence I will try to move to a space that puts me at less risk, such as
.... or .... (Try to avoid incidents in the bathroom, garage or kitchen, near weapons or in rooms without access to an outside door.)

9. I will use my judgment and intuition. If the situation is very serious I can give my partner what he wants to calm him down. I have to protect myself until I am out of danger.

Step two—safety when preparing to leave

If you are going to leave the home you share with your abuser, do so with a careful plan to increase your safety. Abusers can retaliate when they think that a woman is about to leave.

I can use some or all of the following strategies:

1. I will leave money and an extra set of keys with
.... so that I can leave quickly.

2. I will keep copies of important documents or keys at

....

3. I will open a savings account by .... to increase my independence.

4. Other things I can do to increase my independence include

....

5. The number of my local Women's Aid group is .... and the number of the police domestic violence unit is .... I can seek help by calling these numbers.

6. I can keep change for the phone on me at all times. If I reverse the charges from home or use a phone charge card from elsewhere my abuser may trace the calls. To keep my telephone numbers confidential I will use coins or ask a friend to let me use her phone charge card when I first leave.

7. I will check with .... and .... to see who would be able to let me stay with them or lend me some money.

8. I can leave extra clothes with ....

9. I will sit down and review my safety plan every .... in order to plan the safest way to leave the home. I will ask .... to help me review this plan.

10. I will rehearse my escape plan and, if necessary, will practise it with my children.

Step three—safety in my own residence

There are several things you can do to help yourself in your own home. You may not be able to do them all at once but can do them one at a time.

1. I can change the locks on my doors and windows as soon as possible.

2. I can make sure my doors are as strong as possible.

3. I can install security systems, including alarms, additional locks, poles to wedge against doors, smoke detectors and fire extinguishers.

4. I can purchase rope ladders to be used to escape from top-floor windows.

5. I can install a lighting system that switches on when someone approaches my house.

6. I will tell people who look after my children which people have permission to pick them up and will tell them that my partner is not permitted to do so (unless there is a court order saying he can). The people I will tell include:

.... (teacher)

.... (day care staff)

.... (babysitter)

.... (Sunday school teacher)

.... (others)

7. I can tell .... (neighbours), ... (church minister) and .... (friend) that my partner no longer lives with me and they should call the police if they see him trying to get into my house.

Step four—protection with a court order

The following are some steps I can take to make sure that my court order is effective:

1. I will keep my copy of the order at .... (Keep it on or near your person.)

2. I will make sure that my solicitor lets the police know that the order has been made.

3. For further safety, if I often visit another area I will tell the police there that I have an injunction and give them a copy.

4. If I am not sure about the order I will ask my solicitor.

5. If my partner destroys my court order I will get another copy from the court office or from my solicitor.

6. If my partner breaches the order I will call the police, and also tell my solicitor at once.

Step five—safety at work and in public

It is up to the abused person to decide who to tell about the violence. Friends, family and colleagues may be able to help give protection. You should only tell people you can trust.

I will do all or some of the following:

1. I will inform my boss, the security officer and .... at work of my situation.

2. I can ask .... to help screen my telephone calls at work.

3. When I am leaving work I can ....

4. When driving home if problems occur I can ....

5. If I use public transport I can ....

6. I will go to different grocery stores and shops to conduct my business and will go at times which are different to when I was with my partner.

7. I can also ....

Step six—safety and my emotional health

Becoming a survivor of domestic violence can take up a lot of energy and courage. To conserve my emotional energy and to avoid hard emotional times I can do some or all of the following:

1. If I feel down and ready to return to my abuser I can
....

2. If I have to communicate with my partner in person or by

telephone I can ....

3. I can try to use 'I can...' statements with myself and to be assertive with others.

4. I can tell myself .... when I feel that others are trying to control me or abuse me.

5. I can read .... to make myself feel stronger

6. I can call ...., ... and .... as other resources to be of support to me.

7. Other things I can do to help me feel stronger are .... and ....

8. I can attend support groups at .... or .... to gain support and help me build relationships with other people.

Step seven—items to take when leaving

I will consider taking the following items with me when I leave. (Those with an asterisk are the most important. Others can be taken if there is time or else they can be stored outside the home.)

I might keep copies of some of these things outside the home at .... in case I can't take them when I leave. I will try and keep these together at .... in the home, so they are easy to find in a rush.

*identification for myself

*children's birth certificates

*my birth certificate

*social security books

*school and vaccination records

*money

*chequebook and bank card

*credit cards

*keys for the house and car

*driver's licence and car registration documents

*medication

passports

court papers

medical records

rent payment book

bank books

small saleable objects

address book

children's favourite toys or comfort blankets

personal jewellery and photographs

items of special sentimental value ....

Step eight—telephone numbers I need to know

I will find out and either learn or keep somewhere safe, but accessible, the following numbers:

Police domestic violence unit ....

Solicitor ....

Work number ....

School ....

Doctor ....

Church minister ....

Local Women's Aid group ....

Counsellor or support worker ....

Others ....

I WILL KEEP THIS DOCUMENT IN A SAFE PLACE AND OUT OF THE REACH OF MY ABUSER.

Review date: ....

Index

Lion Publishing PLC

If you have enjoyed reading this book, you may be interested in other titles published by Lion. We offer a wide selection of excellent books for both adults and children, publishing for heart, mind and soul.

Titles include:

A Certain Faith: Finding hope in a confusing world by Norman Warren (ISBN 0 7459 1449 7)

A New Beginning: Making a choice for life by Richard Bewes (ISBN 0 7459 1652 X)

A Way With Pain: Overcoming the handicap of constant pain by Mary Batchelor (ISBN 0 7459 1600 7)

A Death in the Family: Practical advice and comfort for the bereaved by Jean Richardson (ISBN 0 7459 2387 9)

Childless: The hurt and the hope by Beth Spring (ISBN 0 7459 3317 3)

Climbing out of Depression: A practical guide for sufferers by Sue Atkinson (ISBN 0 7459 2248 1)

Dying to be Thin: Help and hope for anorexics, bulimics and compulsive eaters by Elizabeth Round (ISBN 0 7459 1952 9)

Experiences of Bereavement by Helen Alexander (ISBN 0 7459 3753 5)

How Can I Forgive? Steps to forgiveness and healing by Vera Sinton (ISBN 0 7459 2010 1)

Is Anybody There? Finding meaning in a confusing world by Dave Martin (ISBN 0 7459 3319 X)

Words of Encouragement: From the Bible
     (ISBN 0 7459 1973 1)
Words of Joy: From the Bible (ISBN 0 7459 1972 3)
Words of Love: From the Bible (ISBN 0 7459 1971 5)
Words of Peace: From the Bible (ISBN 0 7459 1970 7)
Words of Thanks: From the Bible (ISBN 0 7459 1968 5)
You Can Pray by David Winter (ISBN 0 7459 2518 9)

All Lion paperbacks are available from your local book-shop, or can be ordered direct from Lion Publishing. For a free catalogue, showing the complete list of titles available, please contact:

Customer Services Department
Lion Publishing plc
Peter's Way
Sandy Lane West
Oxford OX4 5HG

Tel: (01865) 747550
Fax: (01865) 715152